SQUALL ACROSS THE ATLANTIC

SQUALL ACROSS THE ATLANTIC

American Civil War Prize Cases and Diplomacy

STUART L. BERNATH

UNIVERSITY OF CALIFORNIA PRESS

Berkeley and Los Angeles · 1970

University of California Press
Berkeley and Los Angeles, California

University of California Press, Ltd.
London, England

Designed by James Mennick
Printed in United States of America

For my Mother and Father

Acknowledgments

A NUMBER of people assisted in the preparation of this study. Ralph Roske, Director of the School of Social Science at Nevada Southern University, aroused my interest in blockade-running during the Civil War. Professor Alexander DeConde of the University of California, Santa Barbara, scrutinized the study from its inception and raised important questions which helped shape the nature of my analysis. His continuing interest in the research and writing was both encouraging and flattering to someone whom might have floundered in rough waters. Jay Monaghan, Consultant to the Wyles Collection at the University of California, Santa Barbara, generously shared his knowledge of, and enthusiasm for, Civil War history. Professors Wilbur R. Jacobs and Joachim Remak read the manuscript and made invaluable suggestions. Dr. Ian Mugridge of Simon Fraser University and Mr. Loren Nibbe of Santa Barbara High School most helpfully commented upon portions of the study. Severn Towl of the University of California Press edited the manuscript with diligence, charm, and wit.

The staffs of the libraries and manuscript depositories I visited were invariably courteous and cooperative. Especially helpful were the staffs of the National Archives, the Library of Congress, the Public Record Office, and the University of California at Santa Barbara. The Civil War Round Table of Chicago provided substantial financial aid which enabled me to visit archives from Berkeley to London. The award of the Civil War Round Table Fellowship for 1967–1968 was supplemented by grants from the Department of History and the Graduate Division of the University of California at Santa Barbara.

When ill winds prevented the author from completing the index and reading the page proofs, several good people came to the rescue: Dave Williams and Bill Weber, friends and colleagues at California State College, Long Beach; most of the remainder of the Williams family—Ruth, Janet, and Julie Williams Skotnes and her husband, Andor; Glenda Wadas and Carol Roller of Long Beach; and finally, but far from least, Margery Riddle of the University of California Press.

I would also like to express my appreciation both to Mr. S. W. Higginbotham, Managing Editor of *The Journal of Southern History*, for permission to use material published earlier as "Squall Across the Atlantic: The *Peterhoff* Episode" in *The Journal of Southern History*, XXXIV, No. 3 (August, 1968) and copyrighted 1968 by the Southern Historical Association, and to Mr. John T. Hubbell, Managing Editor of *Civil War History*, for permission to utilize copyrighted material published earlier as "British Neutrality and the Civil War Prize Cases," in *Civil War History*, XV, No. 4 (December, 1969).

S.L.B.

Contents

Origins of the Squall

In November of 1861 a Union naval officer boarded the English mail packet *Trent* and removed two Confederate commissioners. Much has been written about this act, which brought England and the United States to the verge of war. But the *Trent* affair was not the only blow to neutral rights and amicable diplomatic relations. Maritime incidents involving the actions of Union naval officers, the maneuvers of Northern diplomats, and the decisions of American judges as they related to the rights of Englishmen as neutrals at times seriously exacerbated Anglo-American relations. These incidents made for a continuous squall across the Atlantic. They were irritants which, while rarely reaching hurricane proportions, persisted in varying degrees of intensity throughout the American Civil War. Their effects would be felt for many years after.

Curiously, the Civil War prize cases—here defined as the diplomatic and legal cases which emanated from the efforts of United States naval officers to seize vessels suspected of carrying contraband to the Confederacy or of intending to violate the Union blockade of the Southern coast—have not received the attention of historians. There has been only one brief examination of the cases and no comprehensive treatment of them.* The few histories which have dealt with Civil War diplomacy give only meager attention to the cases. Nevertheless, English officials most familiar with the cases and most involved with them appreciated their gravity. They considered the prize cases dangerous to neutral rights and even a threat to peace. The British minister to Washington reported at one point that he was as much or more afraid of the "vexatious proceedings" of the American Navy Department and its officers as factors in bringing about a war as he was of the Confederate cruisers fitted out in England which were decimating Northern commerce.[1]

Trade restrictions have been traditionally among the formidable weapons in a nation's arsenal, for trade provides power and power is what an enemy must be deprived of. On April 19, 1861, six days after the fall of Fort Sumter and two days after the Confederate government invited ships in Southern ports to take out letters of marque and reprisal to prey on Northern commerce, President Abraham Lincoln proclaimed a blockade of the Southern ports from South Carolina to Texas. On April 27 he extended it to include the ports of North Carolina and Virginia.[2]

The blockade was intended to exclude contraband of

* Frank L. Owsley made a pioneer study of the prize cases. His essay emphasizes America's shift from traditional attitudes as a champion of neutral rights to her new posture as a belligerent during the Civil War. My own position is that the significance of the steps taken in maritime matters by the United States to subdue the Confederacy lies more in the character of Anglo-American relations during the war than in changes in America's own viewpoint. Both elements, however, receive full attention in my study. See Owsley's "America and Freedom of the Seas, 1861–65," in *Essays in Honor of William E. Dodd*, ed. Avery Craven (Chicago, 1935), pp. 194–256.

war—goods, such as arms and ammunition, which a neutral is prohibited by international law from furnishing to either belligerent—from the essentially agricultural South and to prevent the exportation of cotton, the principal source of Southern income and the means by which the Confederacy could pay for the supplies it would need so desperately.* Secretary of the Navy Gideon Welles put it simply: the aim of the blockade was "to distress and cripple the states in insurrection." [3]

In its neutrality proclamation of May 13, 1861, the English government warned its subjects against violating either English or international law in derogation of their duty as neutrals. The proclamation was directed specifically against Englishmen who would violate a blockade established by ei-

---

* The term "international law" refers to the body of customary and conventional rules which are presumably considered legally binding by civilized nations in their intercourse with each other. Because of the lack of a centralized supervisory agency, national states interpret and enforce international law in their own way.

The Union government's interpretation of goods considered contraband did not, on the whole, deviate from that of England and other Western nations. Neither the Department of State nor the Navy Department provided any list of contraband items, but the Treasury Department prepared such a list in May 1862 for its collectors of customs. This list included commodities generally accepted as contraband such as cannons, mortars, pistols, bombs, grenades, gunpowder, sulphur, saltpeter, percussion caps, bullets, swords, swordbelts, pikes, helmets, saddles and bridles, clothing adapted for uniforms, masts, ship timber, tar and pitch, and enemy dispatches. In June 1865 President Andrew Johnson listed the following commodities as contraband of war: arms, ammunition, all articles from which ammunition is made, and gray uniforms and cloth. Neither the decrees of the Union courts nor the actions of Northern naval officers suggested that their interpretations of contraband conflicted with those of the Treasury and Executive Departments. Carlton Savage, *Policy of the United States Toward Maritime Commerce in War* (2 vols., Washington, D.C., 1934), I, 90 and 446; James D. Richardson, ed., *A Compilation of the Messages and Papers of the Presidents, 1789–1897* (10 vols., Washington, D.C., 1896–1899), VI, 317.

4 · *Squall Across the Atlantic*

ther belligerent or who would carry contraband to either party. Those who ignored the warning would subject themselves to the penal consequences of the law of nations and to the "high displeasure" of the Queen.[4]

There was general agreement among nations, reflected in the treaties on international law, that neutral governments could not engage in blockade-running and contraband trade, but that they were not required by international law to prevent their subjects from engaging in them. Neutral subjects involved in the illicit trade exposed their property to seizure by belligerent warships and to confiscation by belligerent prize courts. If a neutral violated a lawful blockade, his vessel was subject to condemnation. If the owners of the cargo were identical with the owners of the ship or if they were aware of the existence of the blockade, the cargo was also condemned. The carriage of contraband articles to the enemy always subjected those articles to confiscation. But unless the vessel's owners also owned the contraband, attempted to defraud the belligerent by falsifying the ship's papers, or resisted a search, the ship would be restored.[5]

Numerous British subjects were unimpressed by their government's warning. Lord Russell, the English foreign secretary, reported that Englishmen would, "if money were to be made by it, send supplies even to hell at the risk of burning their sails." [6] It was not necessary for British shippers to go to such lengths, for they could make profits ranging from 300 per cent to 1,000 per cent merely by sending their cargoes to the Confederate States of America.[7]

Sailors who shipped aboard blockade-runners, like owners of vessels and cargoes, did so for the money involved, although some men were undoubtedly attracted by the adventurous character of a voyage through the blockade. Before the war the captain of a merchantman might make a salary of $150 per month; in 1864 he could make $5,000 per month as a

blockade-runner.[8] The attitude of those who ran the blockade is best summed up in one of their popular toasts:

The Confederates that produce the cotton; the Yankees that maintain the blockade and keep up the price of cotton; the Britishers
that buy the cotton and pay the high price for it. Here is to all
three, and a long continuance of the war, and success to blockade
runners.[9]

Although English merchants and sailors were not the
only nationals interested in profiting from the American Civil
War, Englishmen were of primary significance with respect
to the prize cases. England had the greatest number of men
and ships involved in trade with the South and she was therefore most concerned about the protection of neutral rights.
Great Britain was also "Mistress of the Seas" and therefore led
the way in maritime matters.

Citizens of the United States who wished to engage in
maritime commerce dared not do so for fear of seizure by
Confederate cruisers or, if they desired to trade with the
South, for fear of capture by a Northern blockading squadron. Confederates feared sending their own ships to sea because they were subject to seizure by Union warships as
enemy property. Union and Confederate citizens therefore
made dummy sales to Englishmen, making a nominal change
of ownership, registry, and flag. They assumed that a neutral
classification would bring the protection of the British government. Citizens of the North and South dealt with Englishmen
because their closest ties had been with them before the war
and because they could make congenial arrangements with
them without difficulty. The English government accepted
the transfers as legitimate and, as a result, the English merchant fleet swelled and Anglo-American relations became
more complicated.[10]

Before the Civil War, the United States had usually

played the role of a neutral power and had been a fervent advocate of the unfettered rights of neutrals to trade. Americans had endeavored to modify the belligerent right of blockade and to prevent interruptions in the voyages of neutral ships by promoting the concept of free ships making free goods. American statesmen protested with a passion at abuses of the rights of search and seizure which neutral Americans suffered during the wars of the French Revolution and the Napoleonic era. The United States looked on the rights of neutrals somewhat differently when she became a belligerent during the Civil War.

America had traditionally promoted the doctrine of free ships making free goods, which meant that enemy goods not contraband of war were exempt from confiscation if shipped in a neutral vessel. But in some treaties she took the position that enemy ships made enemy goods. The free ships, free goods concept had not become a firmly established part of international law. American statesmen and judges had occasionally agreed to the more generally recognized idea that the goods of a belligerent shipped in neutral bottoms were liable to seizure and that the goods of a neutral in belligerent ships were exempt from seizure.

England held to the view that enemy goods were subject to seizure wherever found, while neutral goods were exempt from capture. France argued that the flag covered the goods. The two positions were compromised in the Declaration of Paris, signed by England, France, and other leading maritime powers in 1856, to the benefit of neutrals. Free or neutral ships would protect enemy goods, except for contraband, and neutral property excepting contraband was not liable to capture under the enemy flag. Although the free ships, free goods doctrine had been incorporated into the Declaration of Paris, the United States did not adhere to it in writing. America did, however, acknowledge that the principles in the Declaration were recognized rules of international law. As it turned out, the question of free ships making free goods was of only nominal importance during the Civil War. Most Anglo-American disputes concerned cargoes that were contraband or that were intended to violate the blockade.[11]

The single incident in which the question of free ships, free goods arose during the Civil War occurred when the English schooner *Clyde* was seized west of Cuba on the grounds that her cargo of cotton and resin was Confederate property. The British minister in Washington, Lord Lyons, called the attention of the American Secretary of State to America's traditional advocacy of freedom of the seas and recalled recent State Department assurances on the subject. Lyons urged that the principle of free ships, free goods be respected.

The Secretary of State admitted that the United States recognized the relevant provisions of the Declaration of Paris and suggested that the Navy Department issue such instructions as might be required. Nevertheless, the prize court at Key West, where the *Clyde* and her cargo had been sent, released the vessel but detained the cargo because it took the view that a neutral flag did not protect enemy property. There appears to be no record of the release (or condemnation) of the cargo or of the issuance of relevant instructions by the Navy Department. The diplomatic correspondence was brief and, since there was no apparent divergence of view between the two governments, the case must be considered inconclusive and of relatively little consequence.[12]

Under the system as Lincoln set it up, the blockade of a port could not be established until a naval force was posted off shore which would be able to prevent the entrance and exit of vessels. Upon arrival at a port, commanders of blockading ships had to notify the authorities on shore that a blockade had been instituted, and they had to allow foreign vessels already in port fifteen days to put to sea, with or without cargo. After this period of grace the port would be officially blockaded and all outgoing vessels could be captured. When a neutral vessel appeared which had not been warned of the existence of the blockade, a notification had to be inserted in writing on her muster roll by an officer of the American cruiser which met her, together with the date and latitude. A vessel so warned was then subject to capture if caught attempting to run the blockade. As the blockade force increased and the blockade became more stringent, Federal naval officers assumed that the general notice given at the ports rendered it unnecessary to give special notice to individual vessels; they finally discontinued giving special notice and captured vessels without warning.[13]

When an officer of a blockading squadron stopped a merchantman suspected of intending or attempting to violate the blockade or of carrying contraband to or from the Confederacy, he first examined the ship's papers—the register, manifest, charter party, bills of lading, cargo invoices, and letters of advice to the master regarding disposal of the cargo. After examining the papers, observing the character of the cargo, and noting the position of the ship and any other pertinent information, the boarding officer would determine the disposition to be made of vessel and cargo. If he deemed them innocent of hostile character or intent, they would be released. If he had reason for suspicion, he took possession of them as lawful prize of war. The captured vessel was then sent, in the charge of a prize master and crew from the capturing man-of-war, to a Union port where a prize court was located. In the United States this meant a Federal district court. The principal district courts dealing with Union prize cases during the Civil War were located in New York City, Boston, Philadelphia, Providence, Baltimore, Washington, Key West, and New Orleans.[14]

Prize courts were intended to fulfill the belligerent's obligation to neutral states and their subjects by adjudicating the legality of the seizure of ships and cargoes in which the neutrals claimed an interest. A prize master gave notice of his arrival in port to the district court judge or to the prize commissioners of the district and delivered into their hands all papers and documents found on board the captured vessel. Ship and cargo were thereafter in the custody of the court. An attorney for the captor or the government libeled the prize, that is, petitioned an inquest for the purpose of determining the facts. Prize commissioners, officers authorized by the court to conduct the first part of the investigation, then examined the ship, cargo, and all papers found on board to ascertain whether or not the vessel was laden with prize matter. The master, mate, supercargo, and at least two of the seamen attached to the captured vessel were individually questioned in some detail about their knowledge of the existence of the blockade, the nature of the cargo, the destination of ship and cargo, and the veracity of the ship's papers. All evidence taken was kept secret until the examinations were completed, then made available to parties having an interest in the case. Claimants could file affidavits, and arguments were allowed. The court then made its decision to condemn or release the prize, after evaluating the evidence in terms of English and American precedents.[15]

If a court did not condemn a prize, it either restored or partly restored and partly condemned the capture. Judges released vessels and cargoes owned by American citizens, by foreigners, or by neutrals residing in the North, if the vessel was not believed to be carrying contraband to the Confederacy and if it was not caught in violation of the blockade. If there was reason for suspicion, but not enough to condemn a prize, damages and court costs would not be awarded to claimants, although they would be awarded if a prize was judged completely innocent. Either ship or cargo or both were condemned for carriage of contraband or for violation of blockade, as previously mentioned. Property owned by persons residing in the South, whether Confederate citizens or aliens, was always condemned as enemy property.[16]

If a claimant was dissatisfied with a decision of the district court, he could appeal his case to a circuit court or to the Supreme Court. Ordinarily a case meriting it would go directly from a district court to the Supreme Court. If an appeal was accepted by a circuit court and the claimant was dissatisfied with its judgment, he could appeal to the Supreme Court. From the Supreme Court he could turn to the Mixed Commission on British and American Claims, established after the Civil War under the Treaty of Washington, for a final decision. In the majority of cases, however, when vessels and cargoes were clearly guilty of violating international law, owners did not even bother to argue their cases. Few cases went beyond the district court.

A neutral owner of a ship or cargo at times appealed directly to his own government to apply diplomatic pressure on the American government in order that a prize might be released before being considered by a court or even during judicial proceedings. The British government, however, took the view that unless the captor had grossly violated international law, claimants should go through the prize courts.[17] England was in a paradoxical position. In the past, she had pushed the rights of a belligerent to their limits; now she was a neutral power. The English government therefore had to maintain two attitudes which were not entirely compatible. It had to support the policies which it had previously employed regarding belligerent rights and which were now utilized by the United States. These, along with any expansions upon those policies which America might make and which as precedents might be useful to England in the future, were fundamental.

At the same time, England desired to uphold the rights of her own citizens as neutrals.

The effectiveness of the blockade was a question of some importance in Anglo-American relations. For England to challenge the validity and hence the legality of the blockade would precipitate a war with the United States. The seizure of English ships and cargoes by American men-of-war without the justification of a legal blockade would mean that American naval vessels were acting illegally and therefore as pirates, if England wished to look at the seizures in that light. Pirates being beyond the pale of law, England would have had to send the Royal Navy after them. On the other hand, the United States could only have viewed British nonrecognition of the blockade as a measure hostile to its own security. Any forceful naval effort to aid neutral merchants who were supplying the Confederacy would have to be considered an act of war.

One of the provisions of the Declaration of Paris stipulated that blockades, in order to be binding, had to be effective; that is, they had to be maintained by a force sufficient to prevent access to the coast of the enemy. Although this was the position which America had traditionally upheld, the United States had not signed the Declaration of Paris because it did not exclude from belligerent operations non-contraband enemy goods under the enemy flag, if goods and ship were privately owned. The United States nevertheless maintained that an effective blockade was prerequisite to legality and insisted that the Union blockade fitted the description of an effective blockade. But this delineation of the Civil War blockade as being effective was not entirely accurate.

Blockade-runners violated the blockade an estimated 8,250 times, which could well mean that it was only a paper blockade—one that was ineffective and therefore interpreted as illegal under generally accepted rules of international law.

Whether the numerous breaches of the blockade made valid its description as a paper blockade, as the Confederate government insisted, was a question much debated during the war and afterward by historians. But, for the story of the prize cases, the important point is that the English government accepted the blockade as legal. The English foreign secretary instructed Her Majesty's minister in Washington that it would suffice for the blockade to present "an evident danger" on entrance to or departure from a Southern port, and this it did. As long as there was any chance of a blockade-runner being seized off a Confederate port, England would consider the blockade lawful.[18]

It was fortunate that England chose not to insist that the Union blockade was a paper one. No Anglo-American war resulted from the blockade question and the Union war effort was not distracted. England had not been moved by altruism in her decision; the American precedent of a loose blockade would reinforce Britain's major naval weapon, blockade, if it should be needed in the future. In addition, the very inefficiency of the blockade assisted British commerce.[19]

When the British did have complaints, Secretary of State William Henry Seward was the American official who dealt with them. Seward employed whatever arguments best suited the issue at hand, sometimes giving little consideration to the principles of maritime law; his primary concern was to prevent Englishmen from assisting the South. In dealing with the British, he had to keep in mind the effect of his statements on Northern public opinion, and he formulated his correspondence in such a way as to raise Union morale and to solidify Northern opinion. Seward aimed at a Union victory over the Confederacy and the avoidance of a war with England.[20]

In the disagreements over the exercise of the belligerent rights of search and seizure, the Secretary of State had no consistent policy line. At first he accepted the liberal interpretations of neutral rights that the United States as a neutral had sought to incorporate into international law. He assured England that America would observe the principles of free ships making free goods; that neutral non-contraband property would be exempt from seizure in enemy vessels; and that English ships would not be unduly interfered with. Nevertheless, when it became apparent that English merchants and sailors were playing a central role in blockade-running, Seward gave fewer assurances and more warnings about the measures which the Union navy would have to take.

Because of Seward's desire to avoid a conflict with England, he proceeded cautiously in the disputes which arose over the exercise of belligerent rights. He did not hesitate, however, to claim full belligerent authority for the United States. In some instances, Seward conceded more than the English government really expected. At other times, he pushed belligerent rights beyond the bounds of international law.[21]

If Seward regarded international law as pliable, Secretary of the Navy Gideon Welles was obstinate in his determination to push belligerent rights to their utmost limits. Welles' preoccupation with achieving victory and his bitterness towards the English government for permitting its citizens to supply the Confederacy impaired his ability to consider the delicacy of diplomatic questions. Welles was inclined to defend naval officers who exhibited more zeal than legal knowledge.

A number of elements contributed to the attitude of Union naval men towards blockade-runners, which sometimes caused them to violate international law. Related to the fact that their job was to capture blockade-runners was their belief that it was patriotic and humane to do so, since it was obvious that every cargo entering or leaving the South benefited the Confederacy or its citizens financially and militarily, prolonging the war, bettering Confederate chances for success, and increasing the carnage. But sailors were also animated by the very natural desire for prize money. When a condemned ship and cargo were sold at auction by a court, the proceeds were split between the government and the captors. One particular capture, for instance, brought a Union lieutenant $8,318.55 and over $1,700 to each ordinary seaman.[22]

Secretary Welles was convinced that Seward had no knowledge whatsoever of admiralty law or of prize proceedings and that he gave in too easily to British demands, thereby staining national honor and relinquishing firmly established rights. To Welles, Seward seemed to have "an itching propensity" to exercise a controlling voice in naval matters with which he had no business. Welles insisted that there should be no State Department or Executive interference in prize matters but that they should be left to the courts. He found support for his position in the Cabinet from Attorney General Edward Bates, himself nonplussed by Seward's interference in his department. It was only with reluctance and under pressure from Seward and the President that Welles submitted to the demands of diplomacy regarding neutral rights. The British Foreign Office was well aware of the differences between Seward and Welles and came to attach great importance to Seward's remaining in office, in spite of his lack of a consistently conciliatory policy toward England.[23]

One potential danger in Anglo-American relations arose from the effort of the United States to supplement the blockade by controlling British trade which passed between American ports and such British possessions as the Bahamas, Newfoundland, New Brunswick, and Nova Scotia. In a sense, this effort was designed to preclude the possibility of British ships and cargoes becoming cases for prize courts. The United States government had reason to suspect that goods shipped from New York and other American ports were ultimately destined for the Confederacy, in spite of their ostensibly neutral destination. A Congressional act approved in May of 1862 authorized the Secretary of the Treasury to refuse clearance to any vessel laden with a cargo destined for a foreign or domestic port if there was reason to suspect that the real terminus for the freight or a part of it was in Confederate territory. Bonds would be required as a guarantee that the true destination was a neutral port, and they would be forfeited if the trust was violated. If a vessel which had been denied a clearance departed, both ship and cargo were subject to confiscation.[24]

The British chargé d'affaires in Washington, William Stuart, soon complained about the enforcement of the act. He denied that the legitimate commerce of a neutral could be interrupted in any way other than according to the international laws of blockade. The American measure, he said, would have to be viewed as "a cheap and easy substitute for an effectual blockade." The act was applied at first only to the New York–Bahamas traffic; Stuart complained that to prohibit trade to British subjects while permitting it to the subjects of other nations was to assume a state of "quasi-hostility" towards England. He therefore insisted that British commerce not be interrupted, except in accordance with accepted principles of international law.[25]

Secretary of State Seward replied that every sovereign state had a right to defend its sovereignty against sedition and insurrection by civil laws and by armed force; it had a legal right to interdict and prohibit within its own borders the exportation of materials useful to traitors. Neutral rights were not involved because no neutral could have a right, denied an American citizen, to act within the exclusive jurisdiction of the United States in a manner forbidden by American law. The statute itself had nothing to do with the blockade, Seward added, because it confined its requirements to transactions occurring in and to persons residing in or being within American territory.[26]

The British countered that the case was not one of domestic legislation, but one in which the forms of domestic legislation were being made subservient to an endeavor to control a particular branch of neutral trade as carried on in the proper territory of the neutral power. Seward repeated the position he had taken earlier and denied that Englishmen were discriminated against since the subjects of neutral states and of the United States were being viewed equally under the law.[27]

British merchants soon found that the bonds which they were putting up to guarantee the shipment of their cargoes to neutral ports were not being canceled by Northern authorities. Lord Lyons, who took over the negotiations on the British side, persuaded the American government to cancel the bonds when the cargoes had arrived at their neutral destinations. But he was soon complaining about fresh restrictions, such as the requirement that bonds be worth double the value of the amount of a shipment. Lyons was able to persuade Seward to lift the American embargo on anthracite coal presumably destined for Canada. Anthracite coal was the fuel most in demand with blockade-runners because of its relative smokelessness. Nevertheless, the Canadian government was expected to prohibit the exportation of the article and its use in seagoing vessels.[28]

English pressure on the State Department to withdraw the requirement for bonds and to admit the falsity of its position regarding the regulation of neutral trade passing through American ports availed nothing. Lyons finally brandished his ultimate weapon. He wrote Seward in August of 1864 that if the blockade of the South could not be rendered efficient without recourse to "irregular and unprecedented methods of harassing and intercepting within the United States the ordinary trade of neutral powers, those powers might well be justified on their part in treating this as a virtual admission that the blockade is not adequately or legally maintained, and in declining under such circumstances any longer to recognize its legality." But Seward knew that, at this late stage of the rebellion, England would not declare war on the United States over the issue, and he conceded nothing.[29]

The United States required victory over the Confederate States, peace with England, and a position supported by international law. To achieve these seemingly incompatible ends, American naval officers, diplomats, and judges should have acted with wisdom, precision, and sensitivity. They often did but occasionally did not. The British government therefore interposed on behalf of its citizens when interference with trade between neutral ports was claimed, when search-and-seizure methods were deemed unduly harsh or illegal, when neutral ports and waters were apparently misused, and when the courts employed doubtful arguments or procedures. Curiously, America's goals were in essence achieved.

2

Could There Be a Blockade?
The *Prize Cases*

THE *Prize Cases*, based upon four captures made in the first months of the Civil War, raised questions which could have undermined the Union war effort if answered in the wrong manner by the courts. The Supreme Court decision was probably the most significant one it made during the war and was one of the most momentous verdicts in the history of the Court's interpretation of Presidential power.[1] The two principal questions presented concerned the right of a government to establish, under international law, a blockade of its own ports during an insurrection, and the right of the President to institute such a blockade in the absence of an act of Congress declaring or recognizing a state of war.

The United States took the position from the opening of hostilities that war did not exist—that there was only domestic insurrection, that there were not two belligerent parties, and that the political integrity of the nation had not been compromised. By taking this view, Union authorities hoped to prevent foreign recognition of the Confederacy and the granting of belligerent rights to its government. If the Northern administration acknowledged the existence of a war, then it could not legitimately deny belligerent status to the Confederate regime or its right to seek help from abroad.

Because of the posture it took, the United States government felt the necessity of defending its use of the blockade, for the right of blockade exists only in wartime and is accorded only to belligerents. Under international law, a nation at war "closes" its insurrectionary ports and "blockades" the ports of an enemy nation. Had President Lincoln simply closed the Southern ports, violators would have been subject to capture like the violators of any other domestic statute. Instead, by proclaiming a blockade, he opened the way for foreigners to recognize the belligerency of the Confederacy. To avoid recognition of Southern belligerency, Secretary of State Seward argued that a nation could employ both belligerent and sovereign rights in suppressing a rebellion and that neither need be granted to insurgents. Because of foreign opposition to this view, the President would not decree Southern ports "closed" until April 11, 1865, after General Robert E. Lee's surrender at Appomattox, when there was no danger of foreign intervention. The technical question existed, therefore, of whether there was an insurrection or an international war.[2]

In fact, European powers did grant the Confederacy belligerent status after the blockade was proclaimed. The Southern government was thereby permitted, for purposes of the war, to possess within its jurisdiction the same powers as if it were in fact sovereign. Acknowledgment of its belligerency entitled the Confederacy to solicit loans, contract for arms, and enlist men abroad, except when forbidden to do so by neutrality laws; to send commissioned cruisers to sea, exercise belligerent rights of search and seizure, and to make use of prize courts; and to have the Southern banner and commissioners recognized as representing a quasi-political community. The United States feared that foreign recognition of Confederate sovereignty would follow.[3]

Closely connected to the North's treatment of the rebellious states and to its relations with neutral nations was the President's conception of his powers in wartime. Lincoln believed in the full use of Presidential power as granted by the Constitution to the Chief Executive as Commander in Chief of the armed forces. Acting under this war power, Lincoln called out troops and directed the enlistment of seamen to suppress the rebellion, suspended the execution of the writ of habeas corpus, issued the Emancipation Proclamation, and directed the Treasury to pay out millions of dollars in war costs —all without prior Congressional authorization. The one unequivocal act which Lincoln took without previous Congressional authority and which would serve as the test for the validity of his interpretation of the war power was his proclamation of blockade. This measure notified foreign nations, in effect, that a war was in progress and that a blockade would be employed to help crush the enemy.[4]

Two Congressional acts touched upon the powers of the President with respect to his control over Southern commerce. On July 13, 1861, Congress granted the President power to close Southern ports and to seize vessels which evaded a closed-port proclamation. This act recognized the insurrection as a domestic affair. On August 6, 1861, Congress passed an act providing that "all the acts, proclamations, and orders of the President . . . after the fourth of March, eighteen hundred and sixty-one, respecting the army and navy of the United States . . . are hereby approved and in all respects legalized and made valid, to the same extent and with the same effect as if they had been issued and done under the previous express authority and direction of the Congress." But the legislation still did not settle the question of whether war existed when the blockade was instituted. Owners of seized vessels challenged the authority of the President to establish a blockade without declaring war. The question was a serious threat to Northern efforts to subdue the Confederacy without granting it recognition.[5]

The decisions of the American courts could have affected the outcome of the Civil War. If the judiciary ruled that the conflict really was war, this would suggest that the United States had recognized the Confederacy through its employment of blockade, and that foreign nations would be justified in doing the same. On the other hand, if the courts ruled that the conflict was insurrection and that no war existed either before or after the action of Congress on July 13, then the blockade would be illegal, prizes would have been taken illegally, and foreign trade with the South illegally broken up. In this case, the blockade would have to be ended, Southern trade would be open, and the rebellion would probably be prolonged indefinitely and might well succeed. The United States government would be liable for huge sums of money in damages, and the psychological effects of such a blow might well have shattered Union morale and the war effort.[6]

The *Prize Cases* involved the adjudication of four ships seized for violation of blockade: the *Amy Warwick*, the *Hiawatha*, the *Crenshaw*, and the *Brilliante*. They were condemned individually in the lower courts; the claimants then appealed to the Supreme Court, where they were judged as a group because the same legal principles obtained.

The brig *Amy Warwick*, seized off Cape Henry on July 10, 1861, by the United States gunboat *Quaker City*, had sailed from Rio de Janeiro at the end of May with a cargo of coffee for Hampton Roads, Virginia. Except for a small portion of the freight which was owned by Englishmen, ship and cargo were the property of residents of Richmond, Virginia.

The vessel was flying the American flag when seized. It was sent to Boston, where the case was adjudicated in the United States district court located there.

The claimants denied hostility to the United States, arguing that the captain was unaware that a war was in progress or that a blockade was in effect when his ship was taken. The claimants also observed that there could be no legal blockade without a Congressional declaration of war. The court, however, condemned the ship and all but the English-owned portion of the cargo on the grounds that any vessel or cargo belonging to persons resident in enemy territory was subject to condemnation if captured at sea. There was no question, the court argued, that a legal war existed, that the President had the right to proclaim a blockade, that the Navy could make seizures under it, that the courts could condemn such captures, or that enemy property was subject to condemnation. The owners of the condemned property appealed to a circuit court, but the original verdict was reaffirmed. The claimants therefore took their case before the Supreme Court.[7]

The bark *Hiawatha* was captured in Hampton Roads on May 20, 1861, by the American flagship *Minnesota*. The bark had sailed from Liverpool for Richmond, Virginia. It reached Hampton Roads on April 23, four days before the blockade was declared, made its way up the river and completed the discharge of its cargo of salt on May 10. The *Hiawatha* then took in a full cargo of cotton and tobacco and, after a two-day delay because of bad weather, lack of pilot and tug, and the breakage of a towline, was ready for sea by May 16. The vessel was English and the cargo was claimed to be English. The prize was sent in for adjudication to the District Court of the United States for the Southern District of New York.[8]

The advocate for the claimants of the ship and cargo argued in the same vein as had been done in the *Amy Warwick* case. Judge Samuel R. Betts, in his official opinion, observed that the master of the *Hiawatha* and the shippers of the cargo from Richmond had received notice of the blockade when they were in Richmond from the British consul there. The master, nonetheless, had commenced taking aboard cargo and had proceeded to lade and dispatch the vessel with intent to violate the blockade by egress. Judge Betts therefore condemned ship and cargo for intentionally violating the blockade by increasing the ship's lading and attempting to evade the blockade after actual notice of its establishment and after the expiration of the fifteen days allowed by the government for her departure. Betts of course ruled in the affirmative on the underlying questions of the legality of the war and the blockade, but stated that he hoped they would be judged conclusively by the higher courts because of their importance to the national interest. The circuit court affirmed the district court decree on appeal, and the case was then taken to the Supreme Court.[9]

The Queen's Advocate General informed Lord Russell that the fifteen days granted to vessels in blockaded ports was a voluntary and liberal concession to neutrals on the part of the United States and, if the *Hiawatha* failed to act within the spirit of that concession, the British government had no grounds for complaint. But since the *Hiawatha* was the first English ship captured for breach of blockade which had come to the attention of the law officers of the Crown, and since the *Hiawatha's* captain apparently had no deliberate design to break the blockade, it would be a gracious act on the part of the United States to release the ship. On the other hand, the Advocate General continued, Her Majesty's government might feel that the captor's claim should be considered first and that the question should be left to the prize court. Russell informed Lord Lyons that the case should go through the prize court without representation, although a delayed decision would be costly to the claimants and Lyons might, if delays should occur, urge the American government to press for a decision or to restore the ship as an act of grace, without judgment.[10]

When the district court decision was made, the Advocate General wrote Russell that the question of the constitutional and legal power of the President to establish and enforce the blockade by his own authority and without the action of Congress was not one which could be considered by foreign governments. It was a question arising under and to be determined by reference to the American Constitution and law exclusively; the Supreme Court would undoubtedly rule on it. The Advocate General found the remainder of Betts' decision acceptable. Russell therefore did not urge Lyons to interfere in the case.[11]

The *Minnesota* seized the schooner *Crenshaw* and her cargo on May 17, 1861, in Hampton Roads for attempting to violate the blockade by egress. The *Crenshaw* had been bound from Richmond to Liverpool and carried a cargo of tobacco. Judge Betts of the New York district court condemned the vessel for having been laden after the beginning of a blockade, the existence of which was known to the claimants, and for having left the port of Richmond more than fifteen days after the blockade was imposed. Betts condemned most of the cargo for being enemy property.

The *Crenshaw* was owned by two partners, one of whom lived in the North and the other who lived in the South. The cargo was owned by parties living in the North, the South, and in Great Britain. Only that section of the cargo owned by Englishmen escaped condemnation as enemy property, and that was because the court assumed that there had been inadequate time for them to have received notification of the blockade. The circuit court affirmed Betts' verdict on appeal.[12]

The last of the vessels involved in the *Prize Cases* was the schooner *Brilliante*, owned jointly by a naturalized American and by a Mexican citizen. Its cargo of flour belonged to the owners of the vessel and to two other Mexicans. The ship had gone from a Mexican port to New Orleans, where it loaded freight which was to be carried to the Mexican ports of Campeche and Sisal. The *Brilliante* was captured by the U.S.S. *Massachusetts* on June 23, 1861, while anchored at Biloxi Bay. The master of the Mexican schooner had intended to request permission to depart, but his vessel was seized and sent to the district court at Key West, Florida. Judge William Marvin of that court found that the *Brilliante* had entered the port of New Orleans after having been warned off and that she was seized while attempting to go to sea in violation of the blockade. He condemned vessel and cargo, and the owners appealed to the Supreme Court.[13]

The decisions made in the foregoing cases by the district and circuit courts affirmed the proposition set forth by the government. A legal war existed, according to the rulings, and this gave to the Northern government the rights and powers of a belligerent with respect to blockade and maritime capture. The decisions in similar cases pending in the lower courts were postponed until the final ruling of the Supreme Court in the *Prize Cases* was made known.[14]

The owners of the vessels and cargoes involved in the test cases pressed the government hard for a decision in the Supreme Court. Attorney General Edward Bates was inclined to move with some speed in the cases, but he accepted advice that it might not be advantageous to act until Lincoln had appointed more politically reliable Supreme Court justices. Bates had also been informed by more than one of the Supreme Court judges that they would be glad if the *Prize Cases* did not come up out of turn and, that if they did come up, that they not be decided until the following term. In other words, the national interest was well served as matters stood; if the cases were taken out of sequence, the decision might damage the Union cause. As a consequence, Bates delayed the hearing of the cases until 1863 and, in so doing, saved the administration from a crushing blow. Even after the President filled the three Supreme Court vacancies (two due to deaths, one to resignation) with Republicans sympathetic to the government's position, the decision sustaining the government was passed by only the narrowest margin.[15]

The cases were argued as a group and, because of their importance, sizable audiences came to hear the arguments before the Court. Richard Henry Dana, Jr., District Attorney for Massachusetts and the man who had ably prosecuted the government's case against the *Amy Warwick* in the district court, again argued for the administration in that case; Edward Bangs of Massachusetts took the side of the claimants. William M. Evarts, adviser to Lincoln on naval affairs at the beginning of the war, and Charles B. Sedgwick, one of the Navy Department's legal advisers, represented the government in the case of the *Hiawatha*, while Charles Edwards represented the appellants as he had in that case and in that of the *Crenshaw* in the district court. Charles Eames, legal counselor for the Navy Department, argued the government's case against the *Crenshaw* and the *Brilliante*, while the firm of Daniel Lord, Charles Edwards, and C. Donahue represented the claimants for the *Crenshaw*, and James M. Carlisle defended the claimants for the *Brilliante*.[16]

The case for the claimants was stated ably by Daniel Lord in his defense of the *Crenshaw*. Lord argued that the conflict between North and South was a civil rather than an international war. Since this was so, the property of persons residing or doing business in the Confederacy could not be seized as enemy property for the reason that the South was still a part of the United States and that only those guilty of rebellion could be considered traitors and hence subject to punishment. Other parties resident in the South had to be considered loyal and their property could not be confiscated. Mere residence did not constitute hostility, and all Southern intercourse with foreign nations was not that of an enemy.

Lord then observed that the power of declaring war in the United States was restricted to Congress exclusively. Until Congress declared war, the President had no power to impose on anyone the character of enemy or to take any measure which could be taken only in time of international war. The power of the President to put down insurrection warranted no legal consequences of war beyond that of the use of force. The President could use artillery on insurgents, destroy buildings which gave them shelter, and occupy places needed for enemy operations; but these steps did not carry the legal consequences of war. If war with its legal attributes did not exist at the time of a maritime capture, then blockade did not exist. When the *Crenshaw* was captured, no American legislation or act of the President provided for confiscation of neutral vessels. There could be no ground of condemnation for breach of blockade. James Carlisle, in his defense of the *Brilliante*, added that Congressional acts passed after the seizures could not retroactively legalize the President's actions.[17]

The case for the government was most forcefully argued by Richard Henry Dana, Jr., whose presentation has been described as an unsurpassed display of "eloquence, passion, and depth of learning." His argument was so persuasive that it gained for the government the crucial support of Democratic Justice Robert C. Grier of Pennsylvania and the Georgia Unionist, Justice James M. Wayne. It probably saved the government from a catastrophic defeat.[18]

Dana put forth the novel theory of "enemy's property" which he had presented successfully in the *Amy Warwick* case at the district court level. The question which concerned him was whether the President was empowered to consider property found on the high seas as prize of war for the sole reason that it belonged to persons residing and doing business in the Confederacy. Dana contended that the right to capture property had no relation to the status or attitude of its owners. It was immaterial whether the owner was a loyal American citizen, an alien, or a subject of the enemy; whether the goods would aid the enemy; or whether the property was on a voyage to or from the enemy's country at time of capture. The fact that the owner of the property was under the jurisdiction and control of the enemy gave the enemy an interest in the preservation and transfer of the merchandise, whether as a source of wealth, taxation and revenue, or of contribution or confiscation. As long as the power with which a nation was at war had an interest in its transit, arrival or existence, the property could be seized as a legal means of coercion.

Dana then dealt with the fundamental question of whether or not a war was legally in progress when the seizures were made. He argued that a preceding act of Congress declaring war was not necessary for the exercise of war powers by the President. War, he said, was "a state of things, and not an act of legislative will." If a war was sprung upon the United States, the President had the authority to meet and repel the attack by every legitimate means, including blockade. Without that authority there could be no protection for the state. The status of war gave the United States belligerent rights—but this did not necessarily mean that the same rights accrued to the Confederacy, for the rights of an area in rebellion were not the same as those of a Sovereign nation.[19]

Dana had done well. The compliments he received from the judges, counsel, and audience were "quite too flattering to put on paper." Justice Grier said that it was the best argument he had heard in five years. Attorney General Bates seemed "quite overcome with his emotions" and Secretary of State Seward was delighted. The arguments of the other attorneys for the government could not achieve the level of Dana's. Sedgwick's brief was uninspired; Eames' was so slipshod and his attitude so frivolous that he made himself odious to the Court; Evarts' argument had its merits, but it lacked the originality of Dana's.[20]

Justice Robert C. Grier delivered the opinion of the majority of the Court on March 10, 1863. Grier was supported in his position by the three Lincoln appointees—Noah H. Swayne, Samuel F. Miller, and David Davis—and Justice James M. Wayne of Georgia. The courtroom was filled with spectators eager to learn the crucial verdict.[21]

Justice Grier first considered the questions of whether or not there was a war in progress at the time of the captures, and whether the President had the right to institute a blockade in the absence of a Congressional act declaring or recognizing a state of war. Grier had no doubts as to whether a war existed when the blockade was proclaimed: "When the party in rebellion occupy and hold in a hostile manner a certain portion of territory; have declared their independence; have cast off their allegiance; have organized armies; have commenced hostilities against their former sovereign, the world acknowledges them as belligerents, and the contest a *war*." With such a war in existence, the government had every right to prosecute hostilities as it would against foreign enemies invading the land. The President was bound to meet the attack "in the shape it presented itself, without waiting for congress to baptize it with a name." Foreign nations had acknowledged the existence of war through their declarations of neutrality; such declarations were only necessary when there were two belligerent parties. Grier said nothing about the sovereignty of the Confederate States.

The claimants argued that the insurgents were not "*enemies*" by being "*traitors*," and that the conflict was not "*war*" by being "*insurrection*." Grier rejected these contentions; the

Southerners, in his opinion, were both traitors and enemies. The majority of the Court, in dismissing the arguments of the claimants, said that it refused "to affect a technical ignorance of the existence of a war, which all the world acknowledges to be the greatest civil war known in the history of the human race, and thus cripple the arm of the government and paralyze its power by subtle definitions and ingenious sophisms."

Justice Grier next considered the question of enemy property, first raised by Dana. The territory in insurrection, Grier declared, had "a boundary marked by lines of bayonets," which could only be crossed by force. South of this line was enemy territory because it was claimed and held by "an organized, hostile, and belligerent power." The property of all persons residing within this territory could be seized as enemy property. The personal allegiance of the owner was immaterial; whatever was useful to an enemy as a potential source of wealth and strength was always regarded as legitimate prize.

Once Grier had settled to his satisfaction the fundamental principles involved, he was free to present the Court's verdict in the individual cases. The Court condemned the *Amy Warwick* and its cargo because their claimants were residents of Richmond, Virginia, and were engaged in business there. Consequently, their property came under the category of enemy property. The *Hiawatha* was condemned because it left Virginia after the expiration of the fifteen days of grace. A vessel in a blockaded port was presumed to have received notice of a blockade as soon as it commenced. The possibility of accidents which might have postponed the *Hiawatha's* departure should have been considered beforehand. The vessel could have left in ample time had the shippers not been so eager to realize the profits of a full cargo. The Court decided, therefore, that the vessel was guilty of breach of blockade.

The *Crenshaw* was condemned for attempted violation

of blockade, and the bulk of its cargo was declared prize because it was enemy property. The remainder of the cargo was restored to its American owners who lived in New York and who had purchased it before the war; they had only been trying to withdraw their property from enemy territory. The *Brilliante* and her cargo were condemned for being neutral property attempting to run the blockade.

Justices Samuel Nelson, Roger B. Taney, John Catron, and Nathan Clifford dissented from the majority position. Nelson voiced the opinion of the minority. He concluded that the war could not have legally existed before the acts of Congress of July 13, 1861, that it was merely a "personal war" of the President. After July 13 the conflict could be accurately described as war. The minority denied the legality of Lincoln's acts from the beginning of hostilities until July 13, when Congress recognized that an insurrection existed. The President, Nelson continued, did not possess the power under the Constitution to declare war or recognize its existence. The power to declare or to recognize a war belonged exclusively to Congress and, consequently, the President had no power to set on foot a blockade. The capture of vessels and cargoes before July 13 for breach of blockade or as enemy property was illegal and void. The decrees of condemnation, therefore, should be reversed.[22]

The minority opinion and the closeness of the vote—five to four—indicated clearly that the conduct of the war might be sabotaged by judges who were more devoted to the South or to their interpretation of the law than to the needs of the United States government. This danger had for some time been apparent, and measures were being taken to rectify the situation while the *Prize Cases* were in progress.

Lincoln and the Republicans decided that the Supreme Court could be more readily relied upon if an additional "loyal" justice was added. A tenth justice, in addition to the three Lincoln appointees and the other sympathetic judges, would make a "safe" Court. It was obvious that the powers and role of the Court rested upon the will of Congress and the President. The legal questions involved in the *Prize Cases* encouraged the administration to act with speed, and the measures taken to pack the Court may have influenced the Court's decision. A bill providing for a tenth justice passed through Congress and was signed by the President exactly one week before the Court made its ruling. The appointment was confirmed on the same day the decision was announced. The Supreme Court could not now jeopardize the Union war effort.[23]

In its most far-reaching implications, the verdict of the Supreme Court upheld the President's claim to extensive emergency powers. The Court supported Lincoln's contention that vast wartime power could be utilized legally. After Lincoln rejected Chief Justice Roger B. Taney's argument opposing the use of the writ of habeas corpus, and after his victory in the *Prize Cases*, the Court made no further attempts to interfere with the effective prosecution of the war. It is likely that the decision in the *Prize Cases* did much to discourage sustained assaults on the validity of the Legal Tender Act of 1862, the Conscription Act of 1863, the Emancipation Proclamation, and the various suspensions of free speech and press. From the time of the decision in the *Prize Cases*, the theory prevailed that Lincoln, as Chief Executive and Commander in Chief, wielded plenary powers.[24]

The Court had used the *Prize Cases* to establish the fact that war legally existed, although Congress had not acted, and that the blockade and capture of prizes in the early stages of the war were legal. The cases were prerequisite to the continued seizure, adjudication, and condemnation of vessels and cargoes seized as prize of war. The Court accorded the Union government full belligerent rights from the beginning of the insurrection, but did not grant any rights of sovereignty to the South. The conflict was considered to be serious enough to warrant giving the North all powers which might be exercised in an international war, while at the same time upholding the rights of the United States as a sovereign nation over the areas in rebellion. The *Hiawatha* was the only one of the *Prize Cases* of interest to the British government; that government agreed that the vessel had been guilty of breach of blockade and therefore did not challenge the Supreme Court verdict.[25]

3

The *Labuan:*
First of the Matamoros Cases

BEFORE the American Civil War, Matamoros, Mexico, could hardly have been described as a vibrant entrepôt. Scarcely half a dozen vessels carried merchandise to and from that port in any single year. One traveler depicted the town as a "used up John Mexican, on his last legs." With the coming of the Civil War, however, Matamoros "presented the very picture of a busy commercial mart . . . the streets, as well as the stores, were piled with bales and boxes of merchandise, and every one you met seemed to be running somewhere, intent on business." [1]

Located some thirty miles up the Rio Grande, across the river from Brownsville, Texas, neutral Matamoros was by early 1862 the great commercial thoroughfare of the Southern states. Mexican officials in the northern states displayed the "warmest feelings of friendship" toward the Confederacy. Wagon caravans transported Confederate cotton across the Texas plains to Brownsville. The cotton was then moved by boat across the Rio Grande to Matamoros. Mexican and Confederaate lighters [barges] then carried the Southern staple from Matamoros down the river, across the bar at the river's mouth, to oceangoing vessels which conveyed their cargoes across the Atlantic to European markets. The manufactured products of Europe traversed the same course in reverse in order to reach the Confederacy.[2]

Private Southern merchants imported both luxury items and necessities of war, but the Texas government was only interested in the latter. From 1862 to 1865 a special state board brought in army rifles, muskets, six-shooters, gunpowder, lead, percussion caps, sulphur, saltpeter, copper, tin, shoes, hats, blankets, woolen cloth for soldiers' uniforms, yarn for socks, and miscellaneous articles such as coffee, leather, rope, and bagging for baling cotton. In addition, it imported medicines and drugs such as quinine, opium, morphine, chloroform, and calomel. The bulk of this trade passed through Matamoros. The Confederate government at Richmond also used the town as a channel for its own trade, for its diplomatic correspondence, and as a way station for its representatives to Europe.[3]

By April of 1863, visitors observed between 180 and 200 vessels anchored at the mouth of the Rio Grande; by late 1864, there were between 200 and 300 ships.[4] By January 1865, the transformation of Matamoros was complete:

Matamoros is to the rebellion west of the Mississippi what New York is to the United States—its great commercial and financial center, feeding and clothing the rebellion, arming and equipping, furnishing it materials of war and a specie basis of circulation in Texas that has almost entirely displaced Confederate Paper. . . . The entire Confederate Government is greatly sustained by resources from this point.*

* S. S. Brown to Lew. Wallace, January 13, 1865, *OR*, Ser. 1, XLVIII, Part 1, 512-513. It must be kept in mind that while the

Officials in Washington early realized that something would have to be done. The Union government, however, was legally harnessed in its efforts to halt the traffic to the Confederacy by way of the Rio Grande. The Treaty of Guadalupe Hidalgo, signed with Mexico in 1848, precluded the establishment of a blockade at the mouth of the river by either party. Since contraband goods shipped directly between a neutral port and that of a belligerent would, according to English and American interpretations of international law, subject a neutral vessel and its cargo to capture and condemnation, neutral traders found safety in importing and exporting goods to and from Matamoros. If a neutral port was the destination of a neutral ship in wartime, neither vessel nor cargo could be captured.[5] The hands of Union naval officers, therefore, appeared to be tied.

Trouble between England and the United States was provoked by the combination of profit-minded traders, Confederates requiring an unhindered trade channel, the geographic location of neutral Matamoros and belligerent Brownsville, a liquid boundary, and zealous naval officers either ignorant of or little inclined to adhere to the principles of international law. Disputes arose over a number of specific issues: the precise location of seizures, the carriage of contraband between neutral ports as a basis for seizure, seizures irrespective of blockade or contraband, American-instigated delays in prize cases, and the awarding of costs and damages.

American Civil War was in progress Matamoros became the main source of supply for the Mexican liberals under Benito Juárez. The town was, however, of far greater significance as a Confederate import-export center. Don Niceto de Zamacois, *Historia de Méjico Desde Sus Tiempos Mas Remotos Hasta Nuestros Dias* (22 vols., Barcelona, 1876–1902), XVII, 514; Kathryn A. Hanna, "Incidents of the Confederate Blockade," *Journal of Southern History*, XI (May, 1945), 221, 228.

In mid-January 1862, the officer in charge of the Gulf Blockading Squadron ordered enforcement of the blockade of the Texas coast between Corpus Christi and the Rio Grande. According to his report, Captain Samuel Swartwout of the U.S.S. *Portsmouth* seized the British steamer *Labuan* off Boca Chica, a few miles north of the mouth of the Rio Grande, on February 1 for being on the Union blacklist of suspected vessels, loading with cotton, possessing no regular papers, and violating the blockade. Nevertheless, Swartwout was uncertain whether neutral vessels could legally take cotton from the mouth of the Rio Grande if their papers stated that they were sent from Matamoros.[6]

On March 5, the British vice-consul at Matamoros, Louis Blacker, inquired into Swartwout's reasons for seizing the *Labuan*. Swartwout replied that the vessel had violated the blockade by loading cotton from Texas brought on board by a rebel steamboat, thereby giving aid and comfort to the enemy. Blacker maintained that the cotton had been dispatched from Matamoros and that the *Labuan* had been anchored off the Mexican coast; Swartwout replied that he did not care: the cotton had come from Texas and he would not be fooled. He intended to seize all cotton and every vessel carrying cotton and violating the blockade; he would even seize a vessel off Tampico, Mexico, if cotton were to be found on board and he knew it to be from Texas. Blacker protested the seizure, but Swartwout was not interested.

Blacker, in a dispatch to the British consul general in Havana, Cuba, described his interview with Swartwout. He also observed that when the *Labuan* was seized, neither Brownsville nor Brazos Santiago, the inlet for Boca Chica, were blockaded and no warning had been given that a blockade was in effect. In addition, according to the Treaty of Guadalupe Hidalgo, the neutral waters of the United States and

Mexico extended one nautical league north and south of the mouth of the Rio Grande. Thus, even if taken off Boca Chica, Texas, the seizure was illegal.[7]

The capture received wide publicity and created considerable apprehension in the Maritime Provinces of Canada and in other commercial centers where traders had been dealing with the Confederacy by way of Matamoros. The British consul general in Cuba reported that the people at Matamoros were so intimidated by Swartwout's threats that pilots and lighters would not go out. There was no service at the bar or at the port, business was suspended, and Matamoros was virtually blockaded by the *Portsmouth*.[8]

When the facts were made known to the Secretary of State, he promised to examine the case carefully and, if the seizure was "manifestly illegal," he would not hesitate to acknowledge it as such, without awaiting a judicial examination. After reviewing the documents, Seward wrote Secretary of the Navy Welles that the capture was apparently without sufficient cause and that the court would probably so decree. In order to avoid a repetition of such cases, Seward recommended that the proper naval commander be instructed to make no more captures of vessels off the mouth of the Rio Grande, unless they were on their way to a Texas port after having been warned of the existence of the blockade. Welles passed the message on to the commander of the Gulf Blockading Squadron.[9]

Seward did not fully inform Lyons of his opinion in the case; instead of expediting the *Labuan's* release, he told Lyons that the case would go through the prize court at New York since a Congressional appropriation for damages would be more certain if based upon the decree of a legal tribunal than if based upon an executive decision without judicial investigation. Three weeks later Seward wrote Lyons that both he and the President had been strengthened in their decision to send the case through the court in consequence of a report from the American consul at Matamoros which indicated that the entire inbound cargo of the *Labuan* had been unloaded at Brownsville.[10]

The British government was unmoved by Seward's evasions; Lord Russell recommended that the Admiralty provide for the security of British vessels and property at Matamoros by sending one or more warships to prevent "undue interference and molestation" by American cruisers. The Admiralty ordered Vice-Admiral Sir Alexander Milne, in command of Her Majesty's squadron on the North America and West India Station, to provide for the security of English vessels and property "clearly and undoubtedly" within neutral waters. The British government assumed that with a respectable naval force in the neighborhood, no flagrant case of violation of neutral waters would occur; if one did take place, Milne was to report to Lyons. Milne was only to use force to prevent recurrent violations if Lyons was unable to obtain redress from the American government.[11]

The attitude of the British government towards the use of force to prevent seizures off the Rio Grande was one of moderation throughout the war. Although a British warship frequently visited the region, there seemed to be little inclination to use force even to prevent questionable seizures. When captures were made at disputed points along the boundary dividing the Rio Grande, British naval officers took the bearings of all vessels seized in order to eliminate any basis for dispute. The English emphasized diplomacy.[12]

Lyons informed Seward on April 23 that Her Majesty's government considered the case of the *Labuan* to be of "very serious aspect" with respect to the interests of the owners of the ship and its cargo, and also to the principle involved which might set a precedent for similar cases. He repeated some of Blacker's arguments, emphasizing that the vessel had been captured at anchor off the mouth of the Rio Grande within the legal limits of the port of Matamoros and that no blockade had existed off Brazos Santiago or Brownsville at the time of capture. He considered it irrelevant that the cotton on board the *Labuan* had been grown in Texas or had, after its purchase at Matamoros, been loaded on board the steamer by a lighter owned by Confederate citizens. Lyons requested the prompt release of ship and cargo with adequate compensation.[13]

Seward persisted in refusing to remove the case from court, but he did urge the district attorney prosecuting the case to speed up proceedings. On May 21, 1862, Judge Betts of the New York district court released the *Labuan* and its cargo. Betts had ruled that the ship's papers revealed vessel and cargo to be neutral property and the blockade of the Texas coast to have been ineffective and thus illegal when the seizure was made. The question of costs and damages was to be decided later.[14]

It had been apparent to Seward for some time that the only way to prevent trade by sea with Brownsville was for the Federal army to take possession of that city. By late January 1862, he was urging this measure upon Secretary of War Edwin M. Stanton. When news of the *Labuan* seizure arrived, Seward re-emphasized the necessity of such a step, pointing out that the Union Navy's right to blockade the mouth of the Rio Grande for the purpose of preventing trade with Brownsville via Matamoros was at least questionable. But Stanton put him off, pointing out that the army was unable to spare troops from more important missions.[15]

Finally, at the end of October 1863, General Nathaniel P. Banks sailed from Union-held New Orleans with the objective of occupying every pass and inlet on the Gulf of Mexico from the Rio Grande to the Sabine River. Banks had no difficulty in taking Brownsville, for the rebels had, as one witness described it, "skedaddled" shortly after the expedition's arrival on the coast; they had had time, however, to set buildings aflame and destroy cotton which had not been moved across the border. By December 28, 1863, the only point from Galveston to the Rio Grande open to blockade-runners was at the mouth of the Brazos River, about 230 miles northeast of the Rio Grande.[16]

The effects of this mission on Confederate commerce were not as detrimental as had been expected. Some of the rebel trade continued by way of Texas through Matamoros, while the rest was merely rerouted further west to Eagle Pass, Laredo, and Piedras Negras. Nevertheless, Confederate problems were aggravated by the occupation of Brownsville and by a withering drought which struck the plains of eastern Mexico and western Texas. These Union gains were nullified, however, when General Banks was ordered north with his army to take part in the Red River campaign. He left only a small garrison in Brownsville, and it was driven out by a small army composed of the citizens of that city in July 1864. Later Union efforts to retake Brownsville failed.[17]

The case of the *Labuan*, however, was far from concluded. A serious misunderstanding had taken place over the question of costs and damages; the charterers and owners of the ship and cargo expected the court to make an award automatically, and the court was waiting for them to apply for the award. The English government, not long after the court's decision on the vessel and cargo, demanded compensation on behalf of the claimants; mere restoration would be inadequate. The *Labuan* was, the English insisted, a neutral ship, "British built, British registered, British owned and manned by a British crew, with a British flag and proper papers, all perfectly regular, with no contraband on board, certified to a neutral port, and making no attempt at concealment or resistance." There was, they added, no justification for the seizure; in fact, that action most flagrantly violated the most unquestionable principles of international law. Seward passed this information on to the prize court at New York.[18]

Nothing further happened until the end of March 1863, when Lord Lyons sent a strongly worded note to Seward, insisting that the matter of costs and damages be settled between the two governments. If Seward permitted the case to go through the prize court and that body refused to grant ample compensation, the British government would be obliged to reject the decision. Seward replied that the claimants had never applied for an award of damages, and that Lyons could hardly expect the court to proceed without such a motion being made. The State Department would have some difficulty explaining to Congress that it had granted compensation to the claimants without their having made application for damages to the prize court. Seward promised that he would instruct the district attorney at New York to notify the claimants or their counsel of an early date when he would move the court to consider compensation.[19]

The Secretary of State was as good as his word, soon sending the promised instructions and even directing the district attorney to prosecute the case to a decision, whether or not the claimants appeared. When, however, Seward learned the size of the claims demanded, he wanted more evidence. The claims appeared so extraordinary that to grant them on the basis of the documents seen might be a disservice to the American public. There was also evidence suggesting that a portion of the outward cargo was contraband; to prove this would, of course, take time.[20]

The British government was indignant; additional investigation into the case appeared incompatible with Seward's professions of good will—nor was it in accord with the usual practice of English and American prize courts. The British persistently and repeatedly urged a speedy resolution of the question of compensation, but Seward ignored the pressure. The British objections would receive attention, he answered; he submitted those objections to the prize court for its consideration, told the British that the necessary testimony had not yet been procured, and said that the claims were so exorbitant that further inquiry was mandatory.[21]

Only after fruitless efforts were made to obtain the necessary evidence did Judge Betts order a special commissioner to ascertain the amount of damages sustained by the claimants. The commissioner did not make his report until 1868, when he estimated that some $190,000 was due to the claimants. The court confirmed the commissioner's report and rendered a verdict in favor of the claimants in the amount suggested.[22]

On April 13, 1868, following a British appeal for payment of the sum awarded, Seward brought the case before Congress in order to secure the appropriation necessary to discharge the obligation. Senator Charles Sumner moved that the Senate consider a bill to implement the decree of the prize court; this motion precipitated a debate which lasted, on and off, for over two years in both houses of Congress. The arguments were typical of those which concerned compensation for illegal American seizures.[23]

Senator William P. Fessenden of Maine and others opposed such appropriations to pay court-awarded damages to British subjects for seizure of their property, contending that England had repeatedly made "open and flagrant war" upon the United States by means of the Confederate commerce raiders constructed in England; there was therefore nothing illegal about the Union Navy seizing English blockade-runners. Regardless of whether or not the American captures were illegal, the British were taking their good time in paying for the damages wrought by the *Alabamas;* Congress therefore was not obliged to expedite the claims of English shippers and merchants. Congress did not appropriate the funds to carry out the decision of the prize court in the *Labuan* case until July of 1870.[24] The appropriation did not, however, bring the case to a close.

The Congressional appropriation covered only the period of detention from seizure to the date of release by the prize court. Damages had also been claimed for a government-caused delay following the *Labuan's* discharge by the court in May 1862, which postponed her sailing from New York to Matamoros. This further detention, lasting thirty-eight days, resulted from the Union government's desire to keep the rebels from learning of the Federal military expedition to New Orleans, then in progress.[25]

The State Department turned the claimants' demands over to the Mixed Commission on British and American Claims, which met several years after the end of the war under the Treaty of Washington. The claimants argued that the detention deprived them of the use of their property, and that while the taking of private property for public use might be justified by the needs of a nation, it likewise involved the obligation to pay compensation. They therefore claimed damages to the extent of $38,000, or $1,000 per day. The Commission unanimously awarded in favor of the claimants on June 23, 1873, eleven and a half years after the original seizure of the *Labuan*.[26]

Many of the issues and problems which arose initially from the *Labuan* seizure were revived and argued again in later Matamoros cases. The precise location of the vessel was never agreed to by the diplomats, one insisting the seizure had occurred in neutral waters, the other neither admitting nor denying it. The situation was similar on other issues. The British made their accusations; the Americans refused to admit the illegality of proclaiming a blockade at the mouth of the Rio Grande, of making seizures before warning that a blockade was to be effected, of the American "paper blockade" at the beginning of the war, of interfering with a neutral vessel plying between neutral ports, or of holding a neutral ship, for reasons of American security, in the port of a belligerent without granting compensation.

Many of these questions had supposedly been settled earlier by treaty or by precedent; none, however, favored the North when the Union split. The prize court ruled in favor of the British in the *Labuan* case, but it provided no explanation for its verdict. Judge Betts neither affirmed nor denied any legal principle upon which neutral traders could rely. Seward's response to these problems was evasion, procrastination, or occasional suggestions for the Secretaries of War and the Navy.

The English government's readiness to send warships to the Gulf of Mexico for the protection of British rights indicated that it expected a continuation of British trade with the South. The American tactics of evasion and delay were perhaps the best means by which neutral traders could be kept in a state of uncertainty, and they were also the best means by which Britain might be persuaded to be more cooperative.

Seward recognized almost immediately the illegality of the seizure, as revealed in his letters to Welles and Stanton, but he nevertheless refused to remove the *Labuan* case from the prize court. He observed that it would be simpler for the British to get compensation if the case went through the regular channels—a possible but questionable explanation. After the court made its decision, no compensation was forthcoming. The reason given was the failure of the claimants to apply for compensation. The court records do not reveal whether or not the claimants were informed that they were expected to do so. When the claims were finally made, Seward found reason for further investigation into the case. When the British continued to pressure the American government, the prize court ordered a special commissioner to examine the claims. His report took over three years to complete. The court ultimately ruled in favor of the claimants on the basis of the report. Nevertheless, the money was not appropriated because of prolonged debates concerning the increased carnage during the war, which resulted from British imports into the Confederacy, and because of extended controversy concerning the highly destructive Southern commerce raiders fitted out in England. When Congress finally voted the necessary funds, other claims resulting from the *Labuan* case remained to be settled—and it took an international commission to adjust those claims. The whole problem of the *Labuan's* seizure might easily have been resolved by Secretary of State Seward at almost any point in the long proceedings, had he been interested in doing so.

4

The Matamoros Cases:
The Union Persists

BEFORE the district court had even considered the *La-buan* case, a similar incident occurred off the Rio Grande. Captain Charles Hunter of the U.S.S. *Montgomery* seized the British schooner *Will o' the Wisp* on June 3, 1862, for having contraband aboard, including gunpowder concealed in fish barrels. The *Wisp*, Hunter observed, was taken on the American side of the Rio Grande about one mile from shore and was sent to Key West for adjudication.[1]

The English naval captain, Edward Tatham, quickly protested Hunter's view that gunpowder landed in Mexico might reach Texas and that this was sufficient reason for seizure of neutral property landing in a neutral port. Tatham, assuming that Hunter had made the seizure in Mexican waters, insisted that blockading cruisers should limit their surveillance to blockaded ports and that their exercise of belligerent rights, in neutral waters, over neutral vessels and property was arbitrary and contrary to international law. The British chargé d'affaires, William Stuart, was not prepared to push so hard. He called Seward's attention to the fact that the *Wisp*, when seized, was in the same location as other ships had been which had discharged cargoes for Matamoros and which had not been captured, and he added that the cargo of gunpowder had been purchased by the military commander of the Mexican government at Matamoros. Nevertheless, Stuart did not make a very strong protest because, unlike Tatham, he believed that the seizure had taken place in Texas waters and that the concealment of warlike goods was most assuredly "mysterious and suspicious." Seward replied to Stuart that it was most likely that the bulk of the contraband aboard the *Wisp* had been bound for Brownsville and that the United States government would not relinquish any of its belligerent rights regarding the halting of contraband trade with the enemy, despite the inconvenience to neutrals.[2]

Judge William Marvin brought this phase of the discussion to a halt by ruling that the seizure had been illegal because there could be no such thing as contraband of war in a trade between neutral ports. But the concealment of gunpowder suggested a possible destination in Texas and hence afforded reasonable ground for suspicion, excusing if not justifying the capture; this suspicion, he ruled, protected the captors against claims for costs and damages.[3]

Under directions from Lord Russell, who had consulted the law officers of the Crown, Stuart protested the court's failure to grant costs and damages. It appeared to the English government that Marvin was correct in his premise that a belligerent had no right to look beyond the immediate destination of articles to a neutral port and to consider what might become of them in a future transaction after reaching that destination. Stuart concluded that the judge's "sound premises ought to have led him to the equally sound conclusion that the captor must pay cost and damages." Seward suggested in reply that if the claimants were dissatisfied they should appeal to a higher court.[4]

When the British government again appealed on behalf of the claimants and suggested that the Executive Department might grant the desired redress, Seward insisted that the case be dealt with by the prize courts. The *Wisp,* he continued, was believed to be only one of many vessels which had cleared from foreign ports, nominally for Mexico, laden with munitions of war and which were attempting to give the impression that their cargoes had a terminal point in Mexico. "The transparency of this fraud, however, is deemed obvious" and the recklessness with which this traffic was practiced was believed to have substantially prolonged the Civil War. Britain was especially culpable in this trade, as it was in building, arming, and manning Confederate cruisers intended to sink and burn American merchantmen. Under the circumstances, Seward concluded, the United States government would make no concessions.[5]

The claimants eventually appealed their case to the Mixed Commission on British and American Claims alleging that they had not been informed of the proper appeal procedures by the American government and that the resulting delay had caused them to suffer considerable losses. The Commission held these statements to be irrelevant and the case to be insufficient, and therefore disallowed the claims.[6]

The Union seizure of the *Will o' the Wisp* infuriated shipping interests in the Maritime Provinces of Canada. A committee of the House of Assembly in Nova Scotia appealed to the British Foreign Office at the end of March 1863 to gain proper compensation for the owners of the ship and cargo; but the English government could go no further than it already had.[7]

The seizure of another ship involved in the Matamoros

trade made it increasingly evident that the United States intended to halt all trade with Matamoros, with or without justification. The English brig *Magicienne* was seized at the end of January 1863, about 390 miles west of the Cape Verde Islands on a voyage from Liverpool to Matamoros. The officer who captured the vessel suspected that it was loaded with goods intended for the Confederates, although he found no contraband aboard. A careful investigation by the district court at Key West resulted in the conclusion that there was "no cause whatever" for the seizure. The district attorney at Key West filed no libel and the *Magicienne* was released, without damages, in early March.[8]

Lord Lyons soon expressed to Seward the dissatisfaction of the British government with the outcome of the case. He noted that there could be no doubt that the capture was "wholly unjustifiable"—the cargo was not contraband, the papers were regular, and the *Magicienne* was not attempting to break the blockade. There was, Lyons added, no excuse for her detention or for denial of damages. He also stated that "the habit of the United States cruisers of seizing vessels on the chance that something may possibly be discovered ex post facto which will prevent the captors from being condemned to pay damages, renders the practical fulfilment of the obligations of a neutral state to respect the rights of the belligerent a task of daily increasing difficulty."[9]

Seward's inquiry of Welles about the case brought the reluctant suggestion by the Secretary of the Navy that a commission might be formed to settle the question of claims. Seward was eager to placate the British, particularly because of the recent crisis over the *Peterhoff* case (to be discussed in the next chapter); he accepted Welles' suggestion and arranged for one American and one British commissioner to settle the claims. The representatives of the two countries agreed to the sum of $8,645. In July of 1866 Congress appropriated the money and the claimants were paid the following month.[10]

On September 11, 1863, Commander Henry Rolando of the U.S.S. *Sonoma* seized the British steamer *Sir William Peel* with 1,000 bales of cotton on board off the Rio Grande. Rolando reported to Welles his reasons for seizing the vessel: she had cotton on board which he believed to be the property of the Confederate States and which was being shipped to England or other ports; she was captured in American waters subsequent to discharging a cargo of contraband articles; she was Confederate property; she was carrying guns and munitions of war intended to convert her into a Southern privateer, and also about 150 axles for field artillery, several casks of iron rings for artillery harness, and two guns. In a private letter to Assistant Secretary of the Navy Gustavus Vasa Fox, Rolando wrote that he could not stand the "hocus-pocus" of the Englishmen, that the *Peel's* master, "a scoundrel of an Englishman," was "trafficking in the blood of my country men" and making money out of America's misfortunes. The *Peel*, Rolando added, would make a splendid vessel for the Union Navy.[11]

Lord Lyons protested the seizure of the steamer in what he thought were Mexican or neutral waters and insisted that there were no grounds for suspecting it of intending to become a privateer; he further maintained that there was not a package aboard that could be considered contraband—legal opinion having been taken before the cargo's shipment from Liverpool—and that the cotton aboard the *Peel* was shipped from Matamoros. Seward referred the note to Welles, but the Foreign Office decided to let the case go through the prize court without further representation.[12]

At this point, the case of the *Sir William Peel* became entwined with the negotiations and judicial proceedings revolving around four similar cases—all British vessels seized on November 4 and 5, 1863. According to the captors, the bark

Science was seized at anchor off the mouth of the Rio Grande, within less than a marine league of the blockaded Texas coast, for discharging her cargo of Confederate-gray cloth—considered by the Americans as contraband of war. The brig *Volante* was also, according to the capturing American officer, seized in American waters just north of the center of the Rio Grande for carriage of such contraband articles as Confederate uniforms, army blankets, boots and shoes. Another officer reported capturing the brig *Dashing Wave* in American waters loaded with a general cargo which included such suspicious items as medicines, blankets, boots, and bales of army clothing. The schooner *Matamoras* was also reputedly taken in American territory north of the center of the Rio Grande, for having discharged spades, boots and shoes, cotton cards, and axes in Confederate territory.[13]

The British government took a different view of the cases. The law officers of the Crown informed Russell that the *Science's* inbound cargo had been legally delivered in Matamoros and that her outbound cargo of cotton was not contraband. In addition, a vessel carrying on a bona fide trade between Britain and Matamoros could not be guilty of carrying contraband. Vessel and cargo should therefore be restored with damages. Lyons should be urged to remonstrate in this and in the other cases. The law officers were not so certain in the case of the *Dashing Wave* and suggested that the owners of the cargo should proceed through the prize courts.[14]

On December 23, 1863, Vice-Admiral and Commander-in-Chief Sir Alexander Milne expressed concern to the officer commanding the United States naval force off Texas about the seizure of ships for carrying contraband of war, after the contraband had been landed. He also questioned the capture of vessels lying in Mexican waters and the taking of neutral ships lying within three leagues of the coast of Texas, for alleged trading with the enemy, irrespective of any question of blockade or contraband. American officers, added Milne, appeared to have misunderstood the scope and spirit of the instructions that they had been given by the Navy Department. A copy of Milne's note was given to Seward by Lord Lyons.[15]

American naval officers received numerous instructions from their government regarding search and seizure. As early as November 1861, Welles had directed the Commander of the Gulf Coast Blockading Squadron, William W. McKean, to prevent contraband commerce with Texas, to exercise "firmly but with proper discretion" the belligerent right of search and seizure, and to capture any vessel carrying articles of war which there was good reason to suspect were intended for the enemy. The use of a foreign flag or the destination to a neutral port was not to shield the conveyance of contraband to the South. More specific instructions followed in April 1862 for officers cruising in the Rio Grande area: all vessels attempting to depart from the Texas side of the river or attempting to enter there were to be seized; vessels endeavoring to go to or leave from Matamoros were subject to visit and search; enemy-owned cargoes leaving Matamoros were to be taken and inbound contraband cargoes were to be seized if destined for the enemy.[16]

When the British government commented upon the serious danger of conflicts between the English and American navies, unless instructions were issued which would modify the behavior of zealous American naval officers, Seward and Lincoln persuaded Welles to issue new orders. On August 18, 1862, American officers were instructed to be vigilant in searching and seizing vessels carrying contraband to the insurgents, but at the same time they were not to seize any vessels within the waters of a neutral nation. Any seizure had to be preceded by a search which indicated that a vessel was carrying contraband to the enemy, directly or by transshipment, or was in some other way violating the blockade. When a naval officer was instructed to proceed to the Rio Grande a week later, he was informed by his superior that his duty to prevent the ingress of munitions into and the egress of cotton from the Confederacy was "of a most delicate character." [17]

On August 8, 1863, the Navy Department issued detailed instructions to its cruisers in Matamoros waters. The new orders made clear that American jurisdiction extended only to the area north of the Mexican-American boundary line which passed through the center of the Rio Grande and then out to sea to the distance of three leagues. All vessels found in American waters were liable to visit and search—and to seizure if found to contain contraband or to have traded directly or indirectly with Texas during their present voyages. American warships were not ordinarily to enter Mexican waters and were not to follow or chase vessels out of Mexican waters. Boats from American warships were not to visit any merchant vessel lying in Mexican waters. A neutral vessel lying in Mexican waters, forced into American waters by stress of weather, could not be visited or searched, even if it carried contraband.[18] If these directions had been followed strictly, there would have been little trouble with neutrals.

Lord Russell, who had received word from Milne concerning the seizure of the vessels and who had consulted the law officers on the Matamoros cases, directed Lyons to make remonstrances to the State Department. Lyons accordingly wrote Seward that the *Sir William Peel* was knowingly seized in neutral waters; that she was seized without search; and that she was seized partly because her homeward cargo was cotton, regarded by the captor as contraband, but not so regarded under international law. Rolando's letter to Fox, intercepted by the Confederates and passed on to the English government, had suggested that the captor was influenced in his proceedings by the desire to acquire the ship for the American Navy.

The British government expected, therefore, immediate restoration of the *Peel*, indemnification to the owners, and a rebuke to be given to the captor.

Lyons dealt less extensively with the other vessels. The *Science*, he went on, even if not seized in Mexican waters, could not be justifiably taken. Its outward cargo of cotton was not contraband and her inbound cargo was bona fide, delivered in neutral Matamoros to Mexican consignees. If trade between England and Matamoros was bona fide, the *Science* could not be guilty of carrying contraband. The *Dashing Wave*, Lyons added, ought not to have been seized before a search had established that she carried contraband or that there were prima facie grounds for capture. The English government required rectification for the wrongs committed in the Matamoros region.[19]

In a second note, Lyons added that Her Majesty's government was under the impression that American cruisers had been directed to seize neutral vessels in American waters for having "traded *simpliciter* with the Confederate States, apart from the considerations connected with questions of contraband or blockade." It seemed that the Union Navy intended to seize neutral vessels carrying goods destined for Mexico which would only be contraband if conveyed to the Confederacy. It also seemed that vessels supposedly carrying contraband on their outward voyage, but which were found to have none on board and which had shipped a return cargo of cotton or other innocent merchandise, were liable to capture. Lyons hoped that Seward would try to clear up the many doubts and difficulties.[20]

On March 9, 1864, Seward made the necessary gesture, though he said nothing specific about the cases under consideration. His reply consisted of a letter from Welles in which the Secretary of the Navy disclaimed the right to capture ships for having carried contraband which had been landed,

unless the contraband had been landed in a blockaded port
and the ships were on the return voyage from such ports; the
right of capturing vessels in neutral waters; the right to capture neutral ships on a bona fide voyage from one neutral port
to another, though laden with articles which would be contraband if carried to an enemy's port; the right to capture neutral ships bound to an enemy's port, not blockaded, unless
such ships have contraband on board; or the right to exercise
exclusive jurisdiction to the extent of more than a marine
league from the American coast. It was possible, Welles went
on, that some commanders were inadequately informed as to
neutral rights; this would be taken care of. But the Texas
coast must be regarded as under blockade and the United
States would claim the right to capture any merchantman violating the blockade.[21]

The law officers of the Crown found the American explanation satisfactory and trusted that the views expressed
would henceforth be acted upon, but they felt compelled to
observe that American naval officers either did not understand
their instructions or had not acted upon them as so explained
—a comment not without insight.[22]

While the two governments discussed the rights of belligerents and neutrals, the United States district court at New
Orleans ruled in the cases under consideration. The *Matamoras, Sir William Peel, Dashing Wave*, and *Science* were released. All were deemed to have been seized south of the line
dividing the Rio Grande. The *Volante*, on the other hand,
was condemned since it was captured a little north of that line
in American or interdicted waters. The claimants appealed the
Volante case, and the United States government appealed the
decisions in all of the other cases except the *Matamoras*. The
Acting British Consul at New Orleans reflected the British attitude towards the cases in his comment on the developments
in the *Peel* case: the appeal was vindictive and the whole case

from beginning to end could only be described as "a piratical outrage."[23]

On October 6, 1864, the British chargé d'affaires, J. Hume Burnley, wrote to Seward, denying any legal justification for the condemnation of the *Volante*. Seizure in American waters was hardly a just reason. Burnley could not understand why costs and damages had been refused to the owners of the *Peel*, and he regretted the intention of the American government to appeal in the cases of the *Peel*, *Science*, and *Dashing Wave*. It was apparent to Her Majesty's government that the seizure of the ships was made upon a false principle, contrary to international law, in which that government could not acquiesce. Although he did not mention it to Seward, Burnley received a letter a week later from the British consul in New Orleans in which it was stated that the verdicts were made on the basis of whether the vessels were found to the north or south of the imaginary line dividing the Rio Grande. The court at New Orleans, it appeared, was entirely lacking in experience in prize matters and, under the circumstances, the judge had "cut a knot" which he had found difficult to disentangle.[24]

Seward consulted Attorney General Edward Bates before replying to Burnley. He then informed Burnley that the judgments of the district court at New Orleans were subject to revision only by the Supreme Court, not by the executive department of the government. The appeals would go forward, in spite of further English efforts to prevent them.[25] The desire to postpone final decisions in the cases and to therefore keep neutral shippers uncertain of their chances of carrying on a reasonably secure trade with Matamoros was likely one of the main motives of the Union government in appealing the cases.

The Supreme Court ruled on the cases in 1867, upholding the district court decision in the case of the *Peel, Dashing*

Wave, and *Science*, and reversing the judgment of the lower court in the *Volante* case. Chief Justice Chase decided that the *Peel* had been taken well south of the Mexican-Texas boundary while passing between neutral ports. Vessel and cargo were, in all probability, neutral-owned. But, since there was evidence suggesting the vessel was in the employment of the Confederate government and that at least part of the cotton aboard her was rebel property, the claimants were not granted costs or expenses.[26]

Chase ruled that the *Dashing Wave* was a neutral vessel bound from Liverpool to Matamoros, with a cargo of general merchandise and coin no part of which was contraband. When taken, the ship was anchored north of the dividing line, with as easy access to the land on the rebel as well as on the Mexican side. This fact and the fact that specie was aboard which was partially owned by someone who may have been an enemy, while not justifying condemnation of ship and cargo, did give reason for capture. Costs and expenses were, therefore, denied.[27]

The Chief Justice decreed that the *Science* and her inbound cargo were neutral property, destined to neutral consignees at Matamoros, and that the cargo had been delivered as consigned. Part of the cargo consisted of Confederate uniform cloth, but there was nothing to show a destination in enemy territory or immediate enemy use. Thus, there was nothing in the character of vessel or her inbound cargo which warranted condemnation. The outward cargo of cotton was presumably neutral property and had to be restored. The *Science* was in Texas waters when seized, but this was no justification for seizure, so vessel and cargo were released, no mention being made of indemnification for the owners.[28]

Chase found the *Volante* to be neutral property regularly cleared from London to Matamoros and the cargo shipped by neutrals in England to neutrals in Matamoros. There were bales of Confederate uniform cloth aboard the ship, but there was no proof of unlawful destination. The brig was taken in Texas waters, but this circumstance alone did not warrant condemnation. However, taken in connection with the character of the cargo, it justified capture. The decision of the district court was therefore reversed, and the court decreed restitution, on payment of costs and charges by the owners of the *Volante* and her cargo.[29]

The *Dashing Wave, Science,* and *Volante* and their cargoes had been sold rather prematurely after the district court decisions, so they could not be restored to their owners. It was not until 1870 that Congress appropriated the funds necessary to reimburse the owners. Delays had occurred because proceeds from the sales of two of the ships and their cargoes had been placed in the hands of a United States marshal who absconded with the funds and in a bank which failed. In addition, postponement of payment resulted from the opposition of Senators and Congressmen who argued that no claims would be paid until certain Fenians had been released from prison in Ireland and until an arrangement had been made for the settlement of the *Alabama* claims.[30]

The owners of the ships and cargoes were not satisfied with the Supreme Court decisions—they wanted costs and damages. They brought their claims before the Mixed Commission on British and American Claims, where they argued that the United States could not legally blockade the Rio Grande so as to interfere with the free ingress or egress of neutral vessels engaged in trade with Matamoros or with the right of such vessels to lie at anchor in the roadstead at the mouth of the Rio Grande while discharging or receiving cargoes on neutral account through the custom-house at Matamoros. They added that trade with Matamoros was a legitimate trade, that the capture of a neutral vessel within neutral waters was illegal, and that there were no such circumstances of suspicion as to afford probable cause of capture, since possession of gray cloth did not constitute grounds for capture. The owners demanded damages for depreciation of cargoes during detention and for the value of ninety-three cases of brandy allegedly removed from the *Volante* while in custody of the district court; and they asked reimbursement for costs and expenses paid by them. The counsel for the United States admitted the legal principles as presented by the claimants, but denied that these principles had been violated in practice or that there were any grounds for costs and damages.[31]

The claims commission awarded the claimants for the *Sir William Peel* $272,920 on the ground that the capture within the neutral waters of Mexico was absolutely illegal and void. The commission awarded $1,785 to the owners of the brandy taken from the *Volante* and $45,684 to the owners of the *Science*, but disallowed the other claims, including those for the *Matamoras*, the latter not having been appealed to the Supreme Court.[32]

None of the Matamoros cases were finally judged to be prizes of war. The *Magicienne* was released without even being considered by a judge. The district court released the *Will o' the Wisp* on the grounds that there could be no contraband trade between neutrals. The court restored the *Sir William Peel* and the *Matamoras* and the monetary equivalent of the *Science* and the *Dashing Wave* because they were taken in neutral waters, but granted no damages because there were reasons for suspicion. These restorations suggest that the naval officers who had seized these ships were either mistaken or lying when they claimed that the vessels were taken in belligerent waters. The district court decisions, apparently made on the basis of the location of the vessels when seized, bore no relation to the rules of international law which held that a vessel could be seized for carriage of contraband to a belligerent or for breaking a blockade, but not for being in neutral or belligerent waters.

The Supreme Court confirmed the fact that the vessels brought before it had been taken in neutral waters, but affirmed the district court's decision to release them on the different but internationally acceptable grounds that the seizure of neutral property passing between neutral ports was illegal. The decision in the case of the *Volante*, condemned by the district court for being in Texas waters, was reversed by the Supreme Court for the same reason it gave in the other cases. The Supreme Court, like the district court, granted no redress because it felt there were just grounds for suspicion in the cases.

Claimants of vessels and cargoes had appealed to the Mixed Commission on British and American Claims in order to recover costs and damages. The Commission rejected the bulk of the claims, although it granted sizable amounts in the cases of the *Peel* and the *Science* and a small amount in the *Volante* case; the American member of the Commission dissented, taking the Supreme Court view that there were adequate grounds for denial of damages. The Commission's award in the *Peel* case was due to the fact that she had been seized in neutral waters, a clear violation of international law. Similar grants were not made in the other cases, perhaps because the Commission was uncertain as to the locations of the ships when seized or because it suspected the intentions of the shippers. No reason was given for the award in the *Science* case, but the *Volante* award was for an obvious theft of British property.

American policy was based on a series of ad hoc acts and decisions. American naval officers made unjustifiable seizures. Seward kept all but the most flagrant violations of international law in the courts while he kept the British at arms' length by making accusations of British culpability in aiding the South and by professing American loyalty to the principles of law to which England adhered. Secretary of the Navy Welles made clear to Lyons the compatibility of the English and American positions, but continued to issue orders which, while becoming more in line with British demands, still upheld the legality of seizing neutral vessels passing between neutral ports if a cargo was ultimately destined for the enemy. The British government came to accept this position, as will be seen in the next chapter, but the American district courts in the Matamoros cases rejected it and released all of the ships.

The district court in the *Wisp* case made clear that there could be no contraband in a trade between neutrals, hence that trade could not be interfered with. The other district court dealing with these cases failed to spell out the position taken in the *Wisp* case, either from lack of knowledge of international law or from an intention to keep neutral shippers wary of trading with Matamoros. The latter was surely the American government's principal motive in appealing the case to the Supreme Court and in Seward's rejection of British demands for redress.

The efforts of the State Department, the Navy, and the judiciary, while seeming to move in different directions, were related to America's goals of victory over the Confederacy and peace with England. Unfortunately, the Union government's immediate goal of preventing trade through Matamoros between the Confederacy and Europe did not succeed. There were only brief lulls in trading following the various Matamoros seizures. In fact, the trade with Matamoros became so active that the Mexicans did not have adequate storage space for all the imports and exports. British diplomacy and the British navy prevented the continued seizures of vessels destined for or departing from Matamoros after 1863. But the American government was not lacking in ingenuity when it came to stifling the Matamoros trade. This ingenuity was reflected in the employment of the doctrine of continuous voyage.

5

The *Peterhoff*:
A Case of Continuous Voyage

LATE in November 1862 the American consul at London, Freeman H. Morse, acquired a copy of a letter privately circulated by the shipping concern of James J. Bennett and Wake of London. This communication announced plans for dispatching a vessel to the Rio Grande. A purchasing agent for the Confederate government was to handle the exchange of the ship's cargo for cotton at Matamoros. Shippers would be assured of large profits. It did not take long for Morse to identify the vessel selected for the mission as the *Peterhoff*, a screw-propeller steamer which had recently run the blockade at Charleston, South Carolina, and had returned to England with a valuable cargo of cotton. He informed Secretary of State Seward of the situation, and the steamer was soon placed on the Union blacklist of vessels suspected of intending to carry goods into the Southern states.[1]

The *Peterhoff* sailed early in February of 1863. Her manifest, shipping list, clearance, bills of lading, and other papers indicated that her destination was Matamoros. She would anchor off the Rio Grande since she was too heavy to cross the bar at the mouth of the river, and her cargo would be transferred to lighters which would carry it up the Rio Grande to Matamoros. Her freight, valued at $650,000, included 36 cases of artillery harnesses, 14,450 pairs of army boots, 5,580 pairs of "government regulation gray blankets," 95 casks of large horseshoes, 52,000 horseshoe nails, iron, steel, shovels, and large amounts of morphine, chloroform, and quinine. The cargo was consigned to the ship's captain, Stephen Jarman, and to three passengers.[2]

After a brief stop at St. Thomas in the Danish West Indies, the *Peterhoff* was captured five miles from that port on February 25 by the Union ship-of-war *Vanderbilt* on suspicion of intent to run the blockade and of having aboard contraband. The *Peterhoff's* seizure was made on order of Acting Rear-Admiral Charles Wilkes, notorious in England for having removed two Confederate commissioners from the English mail packet *Trent* in November 1861, and bringing England and America close to war.[3]

When it had become apparent that his vessel would be seized, Captain Jarman ordered papers burned and a package thrown overboard. He later testified before a prize court that the papers destroyed were letters from his family and that the package thrown overboard was, to the best of his knowledge, nothing more than white powder, as its owner Mr. Frederick Mohl claimed. Unknown to the captors and to the Union courts was the existence of a letter from Mohl to Confederate Secretary of State Judah P. Benjamin, indicating that the package dropped overboard contained dispatches from rebel commissioners in England and France and that the *Peterhoff* mails also contained dispatches. Had this information been known in England, that nation would have had no grounds for protest, for the seizure and condemnation of a vessel carrying enemy dispatches was standard practice according to international law.

The officer of the *Vanderbilt* who boarded the *Peterhoff* asked her captain to bring the ship's papers to the American vessel. Jarman refused, contending that it was impossible since he was in charge of Her Majesty's mail. However, he agreed to an examination of the papers on board the *Peterhoff*. The Union officer studied the papers, considered them suspicious, and seized the vessel. A prize crew took the *Peterhoff* to Key West, Florida, but finding the prize court there closed for an indefinite period, took her north for adjudication.[4]

Prior to the Civil War, American interpretations of international law held that if a neutral port was the destination of a neutral ship in wartime, neither vessel nor cargo could be captured, nor could they be condemned in a belligerent prize court. A belligerent could make no inquiry into the ultimate destination of the cargo once it was landed at the neutral port. On the other hand, if contraband goods were shipped directly from a neutral port to a belligerent, the vessel and cargo were subject to capture and condemnation since transporting contraband to a belligerent or breaking a blockade were illegal.[5]

To enforce the blockade imposed on the South and to frustrate devious traders, Union naval officers broke with American tradition and seized neutral vessels traveling between neutral ports. Northern courts, likewise deviating from the traditional American position, condemned the ships on the basis of the British "doctrine of continuous voyage." Fundamental to this legal concept was the idea that a person cannot do indirectly what he is forbidden to do directly. Thus, as applied during the Civil War, if a ship carrying contraband to a belligerent touched at an intermediate port, that act did not break the continuity of a voyage or remove the stigma of illegality. A vessel like the *Peterhoff*, ostensibly bound for a neutral port, but with an ulterior destination for her cargo in enemy territory, could be seized and sent to a Union prize court for adjudication. If it could be proved that the cargo was directly or indirectly destined for the enemy, vessel and cargo could be condemned.[6] The *Peterhoff* case itself extended the doctrine which, in the cases of the *Bermuda, Stephen Hart,* and *Springbok,* had been applied only to goods intended to be conveyed to the Confederate States by sea, either directly of by means of a transshipment at a neutral port. In the *Peterhoff* case, goods which were designated as contraband by the American courts were ultimately to have reached their destination overland.

The doctrine of continuous voyage had arisen originally as a consequence of efforts to evade the British rule of 1756, under which neutrals were not allowed in time of war to engage in a trade from which they were excluded in time of peace. The American Treaty Plan of 1776 and most subsequent American commercial treaties included what were thought to be safeguards against the effects of this rule by providing that in case of war, the trade of neutrals in noncontraband would be free between belligerent ports and between those ports and the ports of neutrals. Hence, the ultimate destination of a cargo would have no bearing on a case if the freight was carried in a neutral vessel. England would not accept this position.

During the Napoleonic Wars, Secretary of State James Madison made frequent protests against the rule of 1756, and American shippers landed cargoes from the French West Indies in ports of the neutral United States, hoping thereby to break the illegal voyage to France and to render it legal. Sir William Grant ruled, however, in 1805 that the landing of goods and payment of duties in a neutral port did not interrupt the continuity of the illicit carriage of the cargo unless there was an honest intention to dispose of it in the neutral nation. This ruling firmly established the doctrine of continuous voyage in the British interpretation of international maritime law.

After the Napoleonic Wars, American Secretaries of State concluded treaties with various countries which contained provisions for neutral trade from port to port of a belligerent. When Britain was considering rules to be applied during the Crimean War in 1854, Secretary of State William L. Marcy warned that if the British tried to apply the doctrine of continuous voyage, such an act might disturb friendly relations with the United States. Several more American treaties, signed between 1854 and 1861, provided for freedom of neutral trade between belligerent ports. During the American Civil War the American courts reversed their traditional position, as suggested earlier, and decreed the legality of the doctrine of continuous voyage.[7]

Popular opinion in England generally rejected the American legal stand on seizures based on the doctrine of continuous voyage. Captures on this basis had not taken place for half a century; to blow the dust off a doctrine which had become conveniently obsolete in the minds of many Englishmen could only be "illegal"—especially since its employment was now detrimental to British commerce. The British government, however, perceiving a possible future use for America's recognition of the legality of the doctrine, acquiesced in its utilization by American courts during the Civil War.

When news of the *Peterhoff*'s seizure reached England, the press reacted with vehemence. The excitement reached a height second only to that which resulted from the *Trent* affair. Fear of a possible war with the United States caused falling stock prices, and the exchanges closed. Marine insurance rates rose conspicuously, and shipping interests unsuccessfully urged the government to increase the number of warships in the British squadron in the West Indies to give greater protection to their legitimate trade with neutral nations.[8] The *Saturday Review* of London suggested that the North was trying to provoke hostilities in order to escape the humiliation of having to acknowledge openly the military superiority of the South. The London *Observer* typified the view of many in its feeling that the American policy of taking English ships sailing between neutral ports "must inevitably lead to a rupture." *The Times*, London, conveniently overlooking England's introduction and extensive usage of the doctrine of continuous voyage against American commerce during the Napoleonic Wars, attacked its revival and application by the United States as a new doctrine; America was now advancing "extraordinary pretensions." In addition, the journal suspected that the *Peterhoff*, like other vessels seized, had been taken without consideration of destination or cargo, but upon suspicions derived from the ship's name being inscribed in the blacklist. *The Times* ominously cautioned the United States: "There are limits to the forbearance which even a great nation can exercise towards a struggling but still petulant and presuming Government. In the case of the *Peterhoff* these limits have been passed." [9]

Seymour Fitzgerald of Horsham was the Conservative spokesman on foreign affairs in the House of Commons and a leading member of the pro-Confederate wing of his party. He brought the *Peterhoff* case before the House of Commons, criticizing the Liberal government for failing to protect neutral rights. John A. Roebuck of Sheffield was not bound by party ties but, as a consequence of his hatred of the United States, acted as sponsor for the Confederacy in Parliament. He commented that "the conduct of the North American dis-United States has been . . . humiliating to the people of England." Bernal Osborne of Liskeard, a Liberal and a warm supporter of the Palmerston government, did not wish to provoke America and proposed a halt to offensive language under the current combustible circumstances.[10]

The British Foreign Office could hardly ignore the situation. On March 26 the *Peterhoff's* owner wrote Lord Russell, pointing to the illegality of the capture and the necessity for government action to prevent recurrence of such incidents. Russell replied through Edmund Hammond of the Foreign Office that the American government had no right to seize vessels bona fide bound from England to neutral ports "unless such vessels attempt to touch at, or have an intermediate or contingent destination to some blockaded port or place, or are carriers of contraband of war destined for the Confederate States." But the British could not claim any exemption from the right of visit by belligerent cruisers. Vessels suspected of transgressions of international law were clearly subject to capture, and more than a few Englishmen had been found guilty of such violations by American courts during the current conflict. The British government could not "deny the belligerents in this war the exercise of those rights which, in all wars in which Great Britain had been concerned, she has claimed herself to exercise." On the basis of the documents seen, however, the *Peterhoff* appeared to be guiltless, and representations would be made by the British minister in Washington. But if legal grounds for capture were brought to his attention, the case would go through the usual channels—the prize courts.[11]

The London *Shipping and Mercantile Gazette* observed sourly that Lord Russell's opinion favored the rights of belligerents over those of neutrals. Her Majesty's government was reluctant to press neutral rights to a point which might later hinder the exercise of English sea power. The favoring of Northern belligerency could mean advantage to British belligerency in a future conflict.[12]

Russell instructed Lyons to urge the release of the *Peterhoff* and her cargo and to obtain compensation for detention of the ship and her passengers. Lyons had acted, even before receiving the Foreign Secretary's message, on the advice of Vice-Admiral Milne. This officer had warned from the West Indies that the seizure of the *Peterhoff* had aroused great indignation in the fleet. American seizures of British vessels passing between neutral ports on the basis of mere suspicion were becoming intolerable. Lord Lyons received no satisfaction, however. Secretary of State Seward wrote him that the American government did not choose to restore the vessel. The case would go through the prize court at New York, where the *Peterhoff* had been taken, though with as little delay as was necessary. He made no mention of claims.[13]

The British minister was far from pleased with Seward's answer. He informed the Secretary of State that Her Majesty's government could not accept his proposal to turn the matter over to a prize court. Lyons demanded compensation for the shippers, who had been damaged to the extent of several thousand pounds by the unjustifiable seizure of the *Peterhoff* and the detention of their agents. He added gratuitously that there was an impression in England that the American government had decided to stop legitimate trade with Matamoros by means of capture without cause, by delays in adjudication, and by "wanton imprisonment" of masters and crews of ships seized. To pretend that goods carried to Matamoros might be afterwards transported to Texas could not alter the legal character of the trade, for the direct destination of the cargo was Matamoros.[14]

Seward replied that the executive departments of the government would consider the question of claims only if it was not within the jurisdiction of the prize court—and he thought it was. Any negative impression in England of American behavior was groundless. The suddenly-enlarged Matamoros trade had occurred simultaneously with a suspiciously rapid construction of roads across Texas. Southern cotton was passing through Matamoros in exchange for articles needed by the Confederacy. The *Peterhoff* was discovered in this illicit trade and would, with certainty, be handled in the prize court. Nevertheless, renewed instructions had been given to naval officers to be cautious and to conform strictly to the principles of maritime law in conducting searches and seizures. In addition, Seward and Secretary of the Navy Welles decided to transfer Wilkes from the West Indies in order to avoid friction with England. This was helpful in mollifying the British public, which had renewed its outcries against Wilkes when the *Peterhoff* was seized.[15]

The question of mail on board the *Peterhoff* became almost as explosive as the issue of ship and cargo. On April 9 Lord Lyons protested that the vessel's mail had been dealt with in a manner incompatible with the directions given in Seward's letter to Welles dated October 31, 1862. This communication had suggested that neutral mails found on captured ships should not be searched or opened, but sent on to their destination. Prize Commissioner Henry E. Elliott had opened the *Peterhoff* mail bag in the presence of a United States district attorney and against the protest of a British consul. The sealed packages of letters within the bag were not touched. With little delay, Seward telegraphed the American district attorney who was prosecuting the case to "Let the mail of the *Peterhoff* remain inviolate until further directions from me." [16]

The Secretary of State then urged Welles to release the mails, in accordance with his letter of October 31, because of international law, the need to avoid war with England, and the future requirements of America as a neutral. Welles had written in his diary that its "tone and manner . . . were supercilious and offensive, the concession disreputable and unwarrantable, the surrender of our indisputable rights disgraceful, and the whole thing unstatesmanlike and illegal, unjust to the Navy and the country, and discourteous to the Secretary of the Navy." Welles refused to approve release of the mails, arguing that they might contain evidence useful in condemning the *Peterhoff*—which would mean prize money for captors and Navy Department. The Secretary of the Navy was certain that neither Lincoln nor Seward had any right to interfere; the matter must be left to the courts.[17]

Disappointed with the response of Welles, Seward turned to the President. Lincoln asked both secretaries to prepare their arguments and present them to him. This was done, and the President took Seward's side, horrified at the prospect of war resulting from the inspection of English mail. The Secretary of State shortly thereafter informed Lyons that he had directed the *Peterhoff* mails released. A month later Lincoln instructed Welles to order naval commanders to forward captured neutral mails to their destinations.[18]

American newspapers responded to the decision on the *Peterhoff* mails with surprise, regret, displeasure, indignation, and mortification. Except for the most bellicose of Englishmen, British opinion was pacified when the mails were released—and this was the important thing. The *Globe and Traveller* of London lauded Lincoln's moderation and fairness, praising the President and his Secretary of State for staving off "great troubles." Welles, however, was so furious at the outcome of the dispute that a decade later he devoted 38 pages of a 215-page book to reviewing the incident, justifying himself, and crucifying Seward.[19]

Curiously, the British government reversed its position and came close to Welles' way of thinking only two months after the *Peterhoff* mail incident. Lord Russell, in consultation with the Privy Council, the law officers, and several cabinet members, came to a decision which was undoubtedly based on a calculation of the future needs of England as a belligerent. Her Majesty's government would not claim for mail bags and letters conveyed by ordinary merchantmen immunity from detention and inspection by belligerent prize courts; only mail carried by British mail packets would be inviolable.[20]

The seizure of the *Peterhoff*, in addition to all the other difficulties it caused, rendered voyages between England and Matamoros too hazardous for British insurance companies to provide protection—at least until the prize court made its decision on the case. As a result, two Americans went for assistance to the United States minister in London, Charles Francis Adams. They had supplies and munitions which they hoped to send to the Mexicans to help them in their struggle against France. They requested a letter which they hoped would satisfy the underwriters at Lloyd's that their trade was of neutral character and could therefore be safely insured. The evidence they presented convinced Adams that their freight was not intended for the Confederacy, and he drew up a letter to Admiral Samuel F. Du Pont of the South Atlantic Blockading Squadron indicating this fact. The note was thus intended to satisfy Lloyd's and to induce Du Pont to let the traders go on their way if members of his squadron should stop them at sea. Not expecting his note to be published, Adams added some unwelcome remarks on "the multitude of fraudulent and dishonest enterprises" emanating from England. He was pleased to distinguish this one as having "a different and creditable purpose." [21]

One of the American merchants presented the letter to Lloyd's. The firm, infuriated by the note, sent a copy to *The Times*, which immediately published it. The attack was merciless. Ignoring the citizenship of the traders, the newspaper accused Adams of constituting himself as a kind of prize court sitting in London, passing judgment on cargoes before their being dispatched from port of shipment. English merchants had no intention of going as supplicants to the representative of a foreign nation for "licenses" to transact legitimate business. "For the assumption of power in a written instrument by a foreign Minister there has been nothing to equal it since the Legates of the Pope published Bulls, dated from the Vatican, overriding the laws of England." Adams' note, *The Times* continued, seemed to imply that vessels without such a certificate should be captured. The whole proceeding was monstrous.

Other journals recorded similar sentiments, the *Morning Herald's* editorial, for example, being entitled British Submission To Yankee Insults. The *New York Times* did its part to keep British ire aroused: "Certifying to the good faith and honor of British traders, in these days of blockade-runners and privateers, is extra-hazardous. . . . The London *Times*, which in this, as in most other matters, embodies the national wrath and swagger, would do well to turn its indignation upon the real offender. The fact that British shippers apply to Mr. Adams for certificates of character may be a very good reason why *they* should be hung, drawn and quartered—or blown from the cannon of the London *Times*." [22]

Members of Parliament attacked the United States. The Conservative Marquess of Clanricarde, before Charles Wilkes had been removed from his command, said that if British merchants were obliged to American ministers to protect English trade, then "Commodore Wilkes might set a broom at his mast head . . . and proclaim that he had swept British ships and British trade away from the coast." Lord Russell, under pressure from Lloyd's and the shipping interests, found Adams' actions "very extraordinary" and "most unwarrantable"; it was inconceivable for a diplomat to issue such a permit.[23]

Both England and France formally protested. Lord Lyons observed that Adams' note was an interference with

England's legitimate trade since it rendered vessels without certificates suspect and liable to unjustifiable detention and capture. Edouard Drouyn de l'Huys, the French foreign secretary, complained bitterly that Adams had taken pleasure in describing the shippers as having an honorable intent when their vessel was bound to Mexico with arms intended for the killing of Frenchmen. Seward was compelled to disavow the American minister's letter and to apologize for its issuance; only then were England and France pacified.[24]

Adams felt that Seward's apologies were a national disgrace, measures he personally would never take. Nevertheless, Adams had made a serious mistake. He should have considered the possibility that his note might be published and he should have limited his message to the essential information he wished to convey. Instead, he used language which could not fail to antagonize powerful private interests and two national governments. One of his own secretaries in London considered the proceeding indefensible, worthy of "the severest censure." Adams' most recent biographer considers the incident "as the single significant example of imprudence in a mission remarkable for restraint and tact." [25]

The *Peterhoff* case opened on July 10, 1863, in the United States District Court, Southern District of New York. Two weeks later, after the arguments for the government and claimants had been ably presented, Judge Samuel R. Betts ruled that the ship was laden in whole or in part with contraband. The *Peterhoff*, he continued, was not truly destined for Matamoros, but rather for a terminal point in Confederate territory. Betts therefore condemned both ship and cargo and promised that a more extensive opinion would soon follow.[26]

By the time Judge Betts made his decision, British contentiousness on the subject of American seizures had abated somewhat. The American consul in Liverpool, in command of an extensive and effective intelligence network, was inclined to believe that the British government would not be displeased if the *Peterhoff* was judged a prize since it would go far to break up the Matamoros trade and would therefore eliminate problems with the United States. Lord Russell had suggested recently that bellicose members of Parliament wait for the judgment in the cases of the *Peterhoff* and the other vessels pending in United States courts before criticizing the verdicts. He believed that American jurists would act fairly and without intent to interfere unnecessarily with British commerce. The *Saturday Review* confirmed the Foreign Secretary's position, and even the easily excitable *Times* observed calmly that the principles being recognized and extended by the Union prize courts might well be precious to England in some future crisis.[27]

When news of the decision reached Britain, *The Times* saw no need for wrath or indignation and published the refutation of the judgment by the owner of the *Peterhoff* and the brokers for the cargo without a derogatory comment. Only the London commercial interests' *Shipping and Mercantile Gazette* was convinced that American rulings were not sustained by the evidence. That newspaper contended that Judge Betts' "innovation" of basing his judgment on the doctrine of continuous voyage had been done solely to gratify the animosity of the federal government toward England. American journals, not unexpectedly, felt that the decision was entirely sound.[28]

After the law officers of the Crown examined copies of the prize court transcripts, Lord Russell wrote Lyons in Washington that the evidence would not change the position of Her Majesty's government on the inexpediency of any official interference in the *Peterhoff* case. The facts appeared to sustain the verdict. Without positively confirming the judgment, the English government could only suggest that the aggrieved claimants appeal to the United States Supreme Court.[29]

Judge Betts' opinion, covering 104 pages, became available in March 1864. Betts noted that while Captain Jarman had admitted to ordering the destruction of papers and a package once a member of his crew revealed the incident, the descriptions of the items involved differed considerably. Betts was convinced that Jarman had ordered papers destroyed when capture became imminent because they would have revealed that vessel and cargo were liable to seizure and condemnation—that the *Peterhoff* was carrying contraband to the enemy. Although destruction of papers was not sufficient basis for condemnation, it did provide good reason for suspicion when combined with the captain's prevarications.

The nature of the cargo was simple to determine. Most of it was adapted to army use in its present form. If its destination was the Confederacy, the freight had to be described as contraband. When articles of such character were destined for enemy use, all other articles found on the same ship must, despite their innocence, share the fate of the contraband.

What then was the destination of the cargo? Aside from the title page of the logbook, there was nothing substantial to show where the *Peterhoff* was bound. The only testimony concerning the freight's destination came from the sailor who heard a passenger say that it was to be Texas by way of Matamoros. The character and quantity of the articles comprising the cargo were such as to be quite useful to the Confederacy, but were ill-adapted to the Mexican market or the little port of Matamoros. The cargo included, for example, "negro brogans." Such items would be useful in Texas where a Negro population existed, but not in Mexico, where Betts was certain there were no Negroes. Finally, the captain's behavior, erasure of the listing of a contraband item in the manifest, and the failure of manifest and bills of lading to indicate the nature of the cargo and its destination, proved to Betts' satisfaction that ship and freight were headed for the Confederate States.

To exempt vessel and cargo from condemnation because the latter was to pass through a neutral port on its way to Texas would open the door to the practice of fraud upon America's belligerent rights. The ultimate destination of the cargo determined the character of the trade, no matter how circuitous the route by which it would reach that destination. If contraband was to be transported from a neutral to an enemy country, by enemy means of conveyance, the trade was illicit. Under the circumstances, Judge Betts concluded, the voyage of the *Peterhoff* was illegal at its inception. English rulings provided ample precedent for condemnation of steamer and cargo.[30]

Russell wrote Lyons that, after the law officers of the Crown had reviewed Betts' detailed opinion, Her Majesty's government could see no justification for intervention on behalf of the claimants. In fact, the verdict rendered and the reasons given for it appeared to be in harmony with English prize court judgments.[31]

Lord Lyons did, however, ask for a postponement of the sale of the *Peterhoff* and her cargo until an appeal could be submitted by the claimants to the Supreme Court and a decision made on it. Seward replied that this request must be handled by the prize courts. The appeal was made, but before a decision was reached, the district court sold the cargo at public auction for $273,628.99. The Navy Department purchased the steamer for $80,000 from the prize tribunal and used her until March 6, 1864, when she sank off the coast of South Carolina as a consequence of a collision.[32]

In spite of the disposition of the *Peterhoff* and its cargo, the Supreme Court reviewed the case. Chief Justice Salmon

P. Chase made the long-awaited verdict on April 15, 1867, announcing that the *Peterhoff's* voyage had not been falsified; she was on a proper course from England to Matamoros. The vessel's manifest, shipping list, clearance, and other customhouse papers all indicated this fact. Nothing in the evidence showed that the cargo had any other destination. The Court dismissed from consideration the claim that either ship or cargo was destined for the blockaded Southern coast.

Chase observed that paper blockades were illegal according to international law. Hence a sufficient force had to be posted to prevent access to an enemy coast. President Lincoln had proclaimed such a blockade and had explained that it was to extend from Chesapeake Bay to the Rio Grande. But, Chase continued, only an express declaration by the Executive would indicate an intent to blockade the Rio Grande while the United States and Mexico were at peace. In determining whether the blockade was intended to include the river's mouth, it was necessary to consider the treaty with Mexico which stated clearly that the boundary between the two nations passed northwards up the middle of the river. The same agreement stipulated that navigation on the Rio Grande would be free to citizens of the United States and Mexico without interruption by either unless the other party consented. Since Mexico had given no such consent, the blockade could not have included the mouth of the Rio Grande. Neutral commerce with Matamoros, except in contraband, was therefore entirely free.

The Court had decided in the case of the *Bermuda* that an ulterior destination to a blockaded port would infect the primary voyage to a neutral port with liability for intended violation of blockade. The question in the *Peterhoff* case, Chase continued, concerned the consequence of an ulterior destination in a belligerent country by inland conveyance. Cases decided in the British Court of Admiralty in 1801 recognized the legality of neutral trade to or from a blockaded country by inland transportation. It was therefore impossible to hold that inland trade from Matamoros to Brownsville was affected by the blockade of the Texas coast. The *Peterhoff* was destined for a neutral port with no ulterior destination for the ship and none by sea for the cargo to any blockaded port. That cargo, while destined primarily for Matamoros, could reach an ultimate destination in Texas without violating any blockade. Thus, neutral trade to Matamoros, even with intent eventually to supply goods to Texas by way of the Mexican port, could not be declared unlawful. Though clearly inconvenient to the United States if the destination was Texas, nothing could be done about it. The Court judged, therefore, that ship and cargo were free from liability for violation of blockade.

Chief Justice Chase next considered the question of contraband. British and American rulings, he observed, divided merchandise into three classes. The first consisted of articles manufactured, and primarily and ordinarily used, for military purposes in wartime. The second included articles which could be used for purposes of war or peace according to circumstances. The third comprised articles exclusively used for peaceful purposes. Merchandise of the first class when destined for a belligerent was always contraband; goods of the second class were contraband only when destined for the military or naval use of a belligerent; articles in the last category were not contraband at all, though liable to seizure and condemnation for violation of blockade.

A considerable portion of the cargo of the *Peterhoff* was in the third group and did not have to be considered further. A large portion might have been of the second class, but was not proved to have been destined for belligerent use and could not therefore be treated as contraband. Another part was of the first class, or, if of the second, was destined directly for the rebel military service. This section of the cargo consisted of artillery harness, and of articles described in the invoices as "men's army bluchers," "artillery boots," and "government regulation gray blankets." These goods were primarily and ordinarily for military purposes of the enemy. Being of contraband character, destined for a state in rebellion or the use of rebel military forces, they were liable to capture even though destined first for Matamoros. Therefore, the Court was obliged to condemn that portion of the cargo characterized as contraband. Established rules of international law stated that all of the cargo belonging to the same owner as the contraband part had to share its fate. This in effect meant the condemnation of the entire cargo.

Before the Civil War, conveyance of contraband to a belligerent subjected a ship and its cargo to forfeiture. But, Chase said, seizure could now apply only to the contraband itself. The fact of such trade with a belligerent had to be considered, with other circumstances, in determining the awarding of costs. Captain Jarman had failed to do his duty as a neutral by refusing to bring his papers aboard the *Vanderbilt* when requested to do so. His refusal aroused the Court's suspicion. Search of the vessel had led the officers of the boarding vessel to believe that the *Peterhoff* was carrying contraband. It was therefore the duty of the captors to bring the vessel in for adjudication; they could not be held liable for costs by doing so. In addition, the destruction of papers and of a package occurred at the time of capture. Such acts should not have taken place if the destroyed articles contained nothing to prejudice the case of ship and cargo. Considering the other facts discussed and the destination of the ship to a neutral port, with a cargo largely neutral in character and destination, the Court decided not to use the captain's conduct as a basis for condemnation. But the claimants would have to pay the expenses of the appeal if they wished monetary restitution for the *Peterhoff*.[33]

Undaunted by the Supreme Court verdict, the claimants took their demands for compensation before the international commission provided for by the Treaty of Washington. They claimed approximately £67,000 plus interest for the value of vessel, cargo, prospective profits from sale of the freight in Matamoros, and their personal expenses incurred during the lengthy litigation. The claimants in effect asked for a reversal of the Supreme Court decision. The counsel for the United States pointed out that it was not within the jurisdiction of the international commission to judge the validity of a Supreme Court ruling. The commission then disallowed the claims without explaining whether or not the decision to disallow was influenced by the argument of the United States counsel. The acquiescence of the British government through its commissioner in the decision of the commission caused a dispute among students of international law. One of these scholars, Llewellyn A. Atherly-Jones, charged the delegation with refusing to hear the British commissioner. Another, Ludwig Gessner, contended—no doubt with greater insight— that the British Foreign Office had let the matter pass in order that Britain might profit later from the decision.[34]

The Supreme Court's verdict in the *Peterhoff* case had legal significance with respect to contraband, the doctrine of continuous voyage, and blockade. James W. Gantenbein, a writer on the doctrine of continuous voyage, questions the validity of Chase's description of the goods which he condemned as contraband. Gantenbein doubts if those goods were absolute contraband or articles of the first class in 1863. Authorities cited by the claimants indicated that the American State Department, at the end of the eighteenth century, was attempting to limit the list of goods generally characterized as contraband. This effort was realized in agreements with England, France, and several Latin American nations. The contraband lists agreed to were limited in scope and advantageous to the United States as a neutral trading nation; none classified goods such as blankets as absolute contraband. The Supreme Court decision on the *Peterhoff*, therefore, extended the number of articles currently accepted as absolute contraband.[35]

Chase's decision was significant with respect to contraband in a number of other ways. The *Peterhoff* case was the first in which condemnation was based upon application of the doctrine of continuous voyage to conditional contraband —goods usable for peaceful or warlike purposes depending upon circumstances—with an immediate neutral destination. Condemnation of both the absolute and the conditional cargo resulted from the Court's reasonable suspicion that it was ultimately destined for enemy territory. In addition, the judgment was the first to condemn contraband intended for conveyance to a neutral port but then transported inland to a belligerent destination.[36]

The Supreme Court denied the right of a belligerent to extend a blockade to an international river and a neutral port; blockading the Rio Grande would have violated a treaty with Mexico. In practice, however, American cruisers did blockade neutral ports like Nassau in order to make searches and seizures. The Chief Justice also reaffirmed America's traditional denial of paper blockades—though the Union blockade was not at first effective.

The district court decision on the *Peterhoff* case widened America's earlier views on contraband and blockade and reversed her traditional position on freedom of the seas, affirming and extending the doctrine of continuous voyage. The vessel and its cargo were eliminated as a threat to national security during the war. Later cases of a similar nature were usually tied up in court, and neutral shippers hesitated to send vessels even to neutral ports when risk of capture and condemnation was high.

The Supreme Court reversed the earlier verdict of condemnation of the *Peterhoff* but affirmed the ruling on her contraband cargo. Thus the United States acknowledged the legality of the doctrine of continuous voyage with respect to contraband ultimately destined for a belligerent by overland conveyance, but denied its applicability to a vessel. The war had been ended for over a year and a half when this judgment was made: there was therefore no danger to the Union. Any large expansion of antebellum maritime law could not have been to America's advantage since she was once more a neutral.

A study of the major developments in the *Peterhoff* case —Seward's refusal to release ship and cargo, his relinquishing the British mails, Judge Betts' agreement to this release, the Secretary of State's disavowal of Minister Adams' act in issuing a pass to two American shippers, and the decisions in the district court and in the Supreme Court—suggests a single underlying motive behind a series of seemingly contradictory actions—that of national self-interest. The American government wanted victory over the Confederacy, peace with England, and a favorable position in the light of international law. Naval strategy, foreign policy, and judicial rulings functioned together in an often suspiciously silent but curiously sure coordination.

6

The *Springbok:*
A Case of Continuous Voyage

THE MOST heavily criticized and violently discussed Supreme Court continuous voyage decision was rendered in the case of the British bark *Springbok.* The ship had been chartered by Thomas Sterling Begbie of London to take a cargo of merchandise to Nassau. Upon arrival at Nassau, the master was to report to the agent for the owners of the cargo, who would give him orders for delivery of the cargo. The *Springbok* was seized on February 3, 1863, by the U.S.S. *Sonoma* about 150 miles east of Nassau while on a voyage to that port from London. The *Springbok's* officers and crew made no resistance, and the ship's papers were relinquished with no attempt to conceal or destroy them. The papers failed to show the character of the cargo, which was suspected of being contraband.

The prize was sent to New York for adjudication, where an investigation by prize commissioners revealed that the cargo included, among other things, three cases of brass buttons a good number of which were stamped "C.S.A." and "C.S.N.," a case of swords, a case of sword bayonets, eight cavalry sabers, 606 boxes of tin, 1,080 pounds of saltpeter, twenty bales of butternut color army blankets, 47 pairs of cavalry boots and 992 pairs of army boots.[1]

Judge Samuel R. Betts of the United States District Court for the Southern District of New York condemned both vessel and cargo. Betts ruled that the *Springbok's* cargo, some of which he considered to be contraband, was to have been transshipped at Nassau for carriage through the blockade. The carriage of contraband, though broken into several voyages and carried on different ships, would not legalize an illicit journey, even though each of the voyages except the last might be between neutral ports. When contraband goods destined for enemy use were found on board a vessel, all other goods on board belonging to the owner of the contraband had to share the fate of the contraband. In the *Springbok* case, the entire cargo was claimed by the same owners and therefore had to be condemned.

Other factors entered into Betts' decision. The ship's papers, in representing Nassau as ultimate destination for the cargo, were deemed false. Neither the manifest nor the bills of lading mentioned the contraband portion of the cargo and no cargo invoices were found. The character of the papers suggested a desire to conceal contraband cargo destined for the enemy. The master, Betts felt, possessed but denied knowledge of the contents of the cargo. The owners of ship and cargo also had such knowledge and had to be held responsible for intent to carry contraband to the enemy. The fact that the owners of this cargo also owned the cargoes of the *Stephen Hart* and the *Gertrude*, recently condemned in the same court for intention to violate the blockade, added to the guilt of the *Springbok's* cargo. The three cargoes seemed to have been numbered in sequence and marked under a single system. These facts reinforced Betts' belief that the *Springbok's* cargo had the same destination as the two cargoes already condemned.[2]

The Foreign Office and the law officers of the Crown were at first unable to see any grounds for the decree of condemnation, but they reversed that view after examining Betts' written opinion. The British government refused to interfere in the case and suggested that the owners of vessel and cargo appeal to a higher American court.[3]

The district court decision did not escape criticism from other quarters. The *Mémorial Diplomatique* of Paris, a journal which disseminated the views of the French Foreign Office, attacked the decision on a number of grounds. It argued that the ruling was illegal because there could be no capture and condemnation of neutral property on its way from one neutral port to another on the pretext that the property had an ultimate destination to one of the belligerents. Neutral property sailing between neutral ports could not have contraband articles aboard because the designation of contraband only applied to articles bound for a belligerent port. Even if some of the articles aboard the *Springbok* were to be forwarded to the enemy, there could be no legal capture before their departure from the neutral port for the port of the belligerent. In addition, the presence of a few articles alleged to be contraband could not subject an entire cargo and a vessel to condemnation. In any case, the *Mémorial Diplomatique* concluded, there was nothing in the *Springbok's* papers or in the facts of the case which afforded grounds for supposing that the cargo was to be forwarded to a belligerent port. The *Norddeutsche Allgemeine Zeitung*, a newspaper which presented the viewpoint of the Prussian government, made substantially the same criticisms.[4]

The British Foreign Office considered the French opinion worthy of review by the law officers of the Crown. The law officers decided that Laurént Basile Hautefeulle, the principal authority relied upon by the French writer, contradicted most of the principles of maritime law maintained by English and American prize courts and that the quotations from English authorities were misinterpreted. The officers felt that Betts' decision confirmed an earlier British ruling that transshipment of a cargo could not break the continuity of a voyage. This precedent had been established in the first years of the nineteenth century by Lord Stowell, a leading British judge and authority on international law. The legal breaking of a voyage could only be effected by an actual importation of a cargo into the common stock of the country where the transshipment took place. Stowell had also held that a false destination, with contraband on board, subjected ship and cargo to condemnation.[5]

The position taken by the Foreign Office on the *Springbok* decision also came under heavy attack from the English press, as had the original decision. The *Shipping and Mercantile Gazette* led the way with the standard argument that neutral trade between neutral ports was sacrosanct, regardless of the character of the cargo. If the English government could not protect the country's lawful commerce or secure indemnity for illegal detentions and seizures, then the Royal Navy was a vain and useless expenditure; it would be better to declare war against the United States than to let matters continue on their present course. If nothing was done, the trade between Great Britain and her dependencies might just as well be abandoned.[6]

Someone identified only as FAIRPLAY wrote the editor of the London *Globe and Traveller* that it was the true destination of a ship, not the ulterior destination of her cargo, that justified capture. The *Globe* itself insisted that there could be no such thing as a contraband trade with a neutral port. The

London *Standard* considered the district court decision "monstrous," the "spoliation" of Englishmen on flimsy "pretexts." Other journals echoed these views, and the *Morning Herald* of London even described Betts as a "miserable parody of a judge, . . . obviously incompetent." [7] The English government remained unmoved, in spite of the pressure.

The Supreme Court reviewed the case on appeal, and Chief Justice Chase delivered the verdict in January 1867. Chase admitted that while the invocation of documents from the cases of the *Gertrude* and the *Stephen Hart* was irregular, such irregularity could not justify a reversal of the district court decree or a refusal to examine the documents invoked.

Chase then discussed the guilt of the *Springbok*. The Court had ruled in the case of the *Bermuda* that where goods, ultimately destined for an enemy port, were travelling between neutral ports in a vessel whose owners had no connection with this ulterior destination, the ship was not liable to condemnation. The *Springbok* came within this rule, the Court decided. Her papers were regular, and they all showed that the voyage on which she was captured was from London to Nassau, both neutral ports. Her owners were neutrals who appeared to have no interest in the cargo nor any knowledge of its allegedly unlawful destination. The papers indicated Nassau as the terminal point for the voyage, where the cargo would be delivered and where the connection between the *Springbok* and her cargo would end. The Court therefore reversed Betts' judgment in the district court and decreed the restoration of the vessel. The Court allowed no costs or damages to the claimants, however, because of a misrepresentation made by the master when examined and as a consequence of his signing bills of lading which failed to state honestly and fully the nature of the cargo.

The matter of the cargo was believed to be quite different from that of the ship. The bills of lading disclosed the contents of 619 packages, but concealed the contents of 1,388. Such concealment was especially suspect because Nassau was a notorious entrepôt and point of delivery for goods to the Confederacy. The reason for that concealment was thought to be the owners' desire to hide from the scrutiny of the American cruisers the contraband character of a considerable portion of the packages. Furthermore, the bills of lading and the manifest concealed the names of the owners of the cargo Thomas Begbie, and Isaac, Campbell and Co.; possibly this was done because Begbie, owner of the *Gertrude*, and Isaac, Campbell & Co., owner of the *Stephen Hart*, feared seizure of the *Springbok* and the condemnation of her cargo, as had been the fate of the other two ships. The Court then went on to consider the real destination of the cargo, for the concealments alone did not warrant condemnation.

The probability of a destination other than Nassau was inferred from the fact that the consignment shown by the manifest and the bills of lading was to order, that is, to be delivered under terms specified by the purchaser or his agent upon its arrival in Nassau. Such a consignment revealed that no sale had been made or was to be made to anyone at Nassau; had such a sale been intended, the goods would probably have been consigned to an established house named in the bills of lading. The fact that the agent of the owners at Nassau was to receive the cargo and follow the instructions of his principals strengthened this inference.

The character of the cargo suggested the nature of the instructions. A small part of the cargo consisted of arms and munitions of war, contraband within the narrowest definition. Another and somewhat larger portion consisted of articles useful and necessary in war, and therefore contraband within the construction of American and English prize courts. A part of the cargo was specially fit for use in the rebel military service—swords, rifle-bayonets, navy and army buttons—and a larger part was well adapted to such use—army cloth, army blankets, and similar goods. The Court had no doubt that a considerable portion of these goods were going to the Confederacy, the only place where it could be used; nor did the Court doubt that the whole cargo had but one destination. Whether contraband or not, a cargo destined to any rebel port had to be condemned, for all rebel ports were under blockade.

The evidence indicated that the cargo was not to be carried to its ultimate destination by the *Springbok;* the plan seemed to be to send it forward by transshipment. Such a conclusion could be based upon the concealments in the bills of lading and the manifest, and upon the fact that Isaac, Campbell & Co. had supplied military goods to the rebel authorities before by indirect shipments and that Begbie was owner of the *Gertrude* and engaged in the blockade-running business. In addition, the *Gertrude* was present at Nassau, probably awaiting the arrival of the *Springbok* in order to convey her cargo to a blockaded port.

The Court concluded that "the cargo was originally shipped with intent to violate the blockade; that the owners of the cargo intended that it should be transshipped at Nassau into some vessel more likely to succeed in reaching safely a blockaded port than the *Springbok;* that the voyage from London to the blockaded port was, as to cargo, both in law and in the intent of the parties, one voyage; and that the liability to condemnation, if captured during any part of that voyage, attached to the cargo from the time of sailing." The decree of the district court with respect to cargo was therefore affirmed.[8]

The Supreme Court decision concerning the *Springbok,* like the earlier decisions in the case, was soon attacked by many distinguished jurists, publicists, and professors of international law. In terms of credentials, the most impressive criticism came from members of the maritime prize commission nominated by the Institute of International Law, which included professors from some of the most prominent European universities as well as current and former legal advisers to several leading European governments. The commission considered the *Springbok* ruling subversive to the established rule that neutral property on board a neutral vessel traveling between neutral ports was not liable to capture or confiscation by a belligerent as prize of war. The idea of determining guilt on the basis of the cargo's ultimate destination could only annihilate neutral trade by subjecting that property to confiscation upon the suspicion that the cargo would be transshipped, rather than upon proof of an actual voyage of vessel and cargo to an enemy port. Every neutral port to which a neutral vessel might be carrying a neutral cargo would become in effect a blockaded port if there were the slightest grounds for suspecting the ultimate destination of the cargo.[9]

Some of the members of the commission wrote extensively on the decision, and other critics added their voices to the attack. Sir Travers Twiss, a member of the commission and a highly regarded professor of international and civil law, regarded the decision of the Court as "a retrograde movement in the laws of war, increasing their rigour against neutrals on the high seas." He criticized what he called the "doctrine of prospective intention" as extending the future operations of maritime warfare over every sea, and he also argued that the judgment violated the rules of maritime prize law—that the ship's manifest and bills of lading were the best evidence of the ownership and destination of the cargo.[10]

Dr. Ludwig Gessner, Imperial Counsellor of Legation at the Prussian Foreign Office and also a member of the commission, reiterated some of the principal criticisms and added that the evidence suggested that the entire cargo was intended for sale in Nassau. Even if a small percentage of the freight had a hostile destination, only the contraband portion of the cargo could be condemned. The extension of the law of blockade by the Supreme Court was monstrous, and it made apparent that neutral property on the high seas in wartime was "completely at the mercy of an unscrupulous belligerent and the arbitrary decrees of his excited Prize Tribunals." [11]

Other critics added still more points: the bills of lading and manifest were made out in the regular form for vessels going from London to Nassau—there was no concealment; the *Gertrude* was at Queenstown, Ireland, on February 3, 1863, not at Nassau; the invocation of documents from other cases was contrary to well-established principles of Anglo-American prize procedure; the minds of the judges were unconsciously warped by patriotic sentiment and by resentment toward England; the decision rested on the fiction that, although the vessel in which the goods were to be carried was changed at the intermediate port, the voyage was the same —but fictions were contrary to international law and hence illegal; the ruling was based on "groundless suspicion, misapprehension, illogical inferences, unfair surmises, and . . . unjustifiable imputations." [12]

In spite of the criticism, the American government was not impressed, and the British government virtually endorsed the Supreme Court's decision: Her Majesty's government refused to interfere on behalf of the claimants of the cargo. The fact that the cargo was to order suggested that no sale was intended to take place at Nassau. The Court was justified in drawing the inference that the cargo was to be transshipped to a blockaded port. The statement of the agent for the owners of the cargo—that he had intended to sell the goods at Nassau—seemed somewhat late in appearing, since it was not presented until after the Supreme Court verdict. The old rules of law no longer applied to the peculiar circumstances of the Nassau trade—the only real market at Nassau was with Confederate agents and blockade-runners. It seemed doubtful whether a suspicious trade with Nassau could be properly construed as a bona fide neutral trade.[13] While the United States was leading the way in expanding belligerent maritime rights, the British government assumed that it was in its interest to acquiesce, and this it did.

The owners of the cargo were hardly satisfied with the conclusions drawn by the British government, and they took their case before the Mixed Commission on British and American Claims. William M. Evarts presented a thorough brief on behalf of the claimants, even stressing the future interests of the United States and the rights of neutrals in general: "If a belligerent prize court can . . . be the master of neutral commerce by this *fiction* of continuous voyage for the case of all trade between neutral ports, which has its stimulus from the state of war, why, then, we have a paper blockade of the neutral ports in question, and their commerce is at the mercy of the belligerent." This Commission, however, unanimously upheld the position taken by the English and American governments and disallowed the claim for the cargo.[14]

As in the case of the *Peterhoff*, the British government through its commissioner agreed to the Supreme Court decision, undoubtedly because that ruling was so favorable to belligerent maritime ascendancy. The awareness of the future use to which the American precedent might be put was considerably reinforced by Britain's experience during the Crimean War, when it was found that the English prize code was unable to prevent vast quantities of contraband from reaching Russia by way of neutral ports.[15]

Because of the controversy surrounding it, the validity and legality of the Supreme Court ruling requires analysis. Critics persistently asserted that American courts held that a mere suspicion of intent to proceed ultimately to a belligerent destination justified condemnation of a cargo or of a ship and cargo. This suspicion, critics said, was based upon insufficient evidence.

American courts did not, however, base their decisions upon mere conjecture. The critics may have interpreted differently the conclusions to be drawn from the evidence, but there was nothing extraordinary about the Supreme Court's approach. The Court did not hold that intention alone was a violation of law; condemnation resulted from what the Court held to be proof of specific measures taken with an illegal intention. The Court ruled that the measures included, among other things, concealment of a contraband cargo and the fact that consignment was to order. If a ship's papers were incomplete, ambiguous, contradictory, or fraudulent, or if witnesses who alone could dispel the suspicious nature of certain circumstances failed to appear before a court, that court could not decline to look beneath a cover of fraud to ascertain the truth. The owners of the *Springbok's* cargo were thought to have had an illegal intention of violating the blockade, and an unbiased examination of the evidence sustains this view.

Nassau, in British New Providence, could not be considered an ordinary neutral port, as the English government acknowledged. It was the most important intermediate port in the West Indies employed by blockade-runners as a point of departure to and arrival from the blockaded coast. Shipowners recognized early in the war the futility of sending large, slow, deep-draft vessels from England to attempt to run the blockade; those ships were too easily captured. Cargoes were soon transferred at intermediate ports to smaller vessels of light draft, specially constructed to run the blockade. Nassau, only 540 miles from the blockaded coast, blossomed as a result of the war, like Matamoros. For most of the war, blockade-runners plied only between the neutral ports and the South.[16]

Until the employment of the doctrine of continuous voyage by the Union, used in order to overcome the disadvantage of having neutral ports near the blockaded Confederacy, shippers carried on under the impression that trade between neutral ports was untouchable. The danger of seizure between a neutral port and a belligerent port was thought to be less if goods for the Confederacy were shipped the shorter distance from intermediate ports than if they were shipped the whole distance from England. A cargo supposedly destined for Nassau, of course, came under immediate suspicion, especially if it contained items of no practical use at that port and of substantial value to the Confederacy.

As mentioned earlier, the doctrine of continuous voyage in essence meant that a person could not be permitted to do indirectly what he was forbidden to do directly; a fraudulent act remained fraudulent and objectionable though concealed beneath the forms of legality. The doctrine did not rest upon a fiction; it looked beneath the fiction to the facts. In this sense, the employment of the doctrine by the United States was only fair to that nation, then in the midst of civil war.

Although the Navy Department issued orders for seizure of neutral ships passing between neutral ports if the ultimate destination of ship or cargo was thought to be the Confederacy, the courts generally rejected condemnations on the basis of the continuous voyage rule. With the cases of *Peterhoff*, the *Springbok*, and several others emanating from the war, the doctrine was utilized. The continuous voyage verdicts made during the war contradicted other verdicts in which neutral trade passing between neutral ports was regarded as inviolable. But this was not considered relevant. American judges ruled as they deemed best. If the Union government had formulated a plan to disorient neutral traders, it could not have chosen a better approach.

In the *Springbok* case, the Supreme Court held that a cargo shipped with an intention of ultimately bringing it into a blockaded port was subject to seizure as soon as it left the original port of shipment; this rule pertained even if the cargo was to be transshipped at an intermediate port, and the vessel in which it was found when captured was not the one which was to carry it to a blockaded port. The Court applied fully the penalty of breach of blockade to a guilty cargo in an innocent ship; it was the first case in which a vessel was released while its cargo was condemned for intended breach of blockade. This application of the doctrine of continuous voyage was foreshadowed in the Supreme Court rulings in the cases of the *Stephen Hart* and the *Bermuda,* but in those cases the vessel was condemned along with the cargo.[17]

As in the *Peterhoff* case, the Supreme Court ruling made apparent that the United States government was discarding those rules pertaining to neutral rights for which it had made war in 1812 and which it had upheld since then. The first of these was that there was to have been no confiscation of noncontraband goods owned by neutrals and taken in neutral ships on the ground that such goods might be transshipped at an intermediate port to an enemy port. Second, blockades had to be of specific ports, not of the enemy coastline in general, as the doctrine of continuous voyage permitted. The *Springbok* and other continuous voyage rulings went far towards making a blockade of enemy ports unnecessary by substituting what at times amounted to a paper blockade of neutral ports.[18]

The change in American legal thinking and the expansion of English doctrine by American courts seemed immoral to some and illegal to others. But what took place was merely the application of a well-established principle to a new state of facts—the doctrine of continuous voyage applied and expanded to meet the needs of the United States during its Civil War.

A change in circumstances, the employment for the first time of fast steam-driven vessels designed to run a blockade, departures of neutral vessels and cargoes from neutral ports close to an enemy, neutral cargoes arriving at a port directly across the border from an enemy and intended for that enemy —all of these factors influenced the decision to utilize advantageously the doctrine of continuous voyage. Changed circumstances meant changed practices, and changed practices meant changed principles. The governments of the United States and England recognized these facts during the Civil War—and the principles of international law are drawn from the practice of nations rather than from the writings of theorists when the two are at variance.[19]

7

The Violation of
Neutral Territory

THE EMPLOYMENT of new legal interpretations during the Civil War was not the only step the Union government took which raised foreign eyebrows. According to international law as generally interpreted in the 1860's, belligerent
operations could not take place within the one league or
three-mile limit of national sovereignty extending off the
shore of neutral territories. Nevertheless, the governments of
England, Spain, and Denmark were obliged to protest against
the operations of Union naval officers whom they accused of
violating neutral sovereignty. The charges included the chasing of, firing upon, and burning and seizing suspected blockade-runners in neutral territory, as well as the following of
suspected vessels from neutral ports in order to make captures, and the blockading of neutral ports.

The American government recognized the illegality of
such measures, but the Secretary of the Navy only reluctantly

reprimanded the officers involved, and only the minimum demands of foreign powers were met by the Secretary of State. The violation of neutral territory was one of the side effects of a determination to obtain prize money and to win the war. Such encroachments, although not national policy, were tacitly accepted by the American government. England had often violated neutral territory during the Napoleonic Wars and the United States had protested loudly; when the United States became the principal maritime belligerent a half-century later, she hardly set an appropriate example.

The Navy Department issued adequate directions for its officers to respect the jurisdiction of neutrals. In June of 1862, for example, Welles ordered the Commander of the East Gulf Blockading Squadron to impress upon his officers the necessity of respecting Spanish territorial sovereignty; they "should not chase, fire upon, board or seize vessels within the territorial waters of Cuba." The Commander followed his orders, but his officers did not always follow theirs.[1]

Shortly after the foregoing orders had been issued, the United States Department of State received protests from both Spain and England about the affair of the *Blanche*, a steamer of English registry which was destroyed in Cuban waters on October 7, 1862, while on its way from Lavaca, Texas, to Havana, subsequent to a chase by an American warship. According to the captain of the *Blanche* and two members of his crew, the U.S.S. *Montgomery* under command of Captain Charles Hunter chased the *Blanche* while she was in Cuban waters and while showing the British ensign. The *Blanche* then anchored about 300 yards off Marianao Beach. Her pilot went ashore and returned with the Spanish *alcade de mar* and his son. The Spanish official hoisted the Spanish flag over the Union Jack to show that the *Blanche* was under the protection of the authority and within the jurisdiction of the queen of Spain.

Two boats full of armed men approached the *Blanche*, according to the report, and the *Blanche's* captain, in order to save his ship and cargo, ran his vessel aground. The Americans then boarded the *Blanche* and took possession of her. The Spanish official protested in Spanish against the violation of neutral territory and the insult to his country's flag. The boarding officer, so the report went, replied that he didn't care about Spanish authority or flags, and he ordered the *alcalde* to leave the ship. Since the Spanish official did not comply immediately, he was forced to the side of the ship and one of the men struck his son in the face. The *alcalde* and his son were then compelled to get into their own boat, at the same time receiving abuse and threats from the Americans. A few minutes later it was discovered that the *Blanche* was afire, the conflagration allegedly started by the Americans. When someone cried out that there was gunpowder aboard, the Americans rushed for their boats, taking with them the Spanish pilot and one of the passengers of the *Blanche*. The crew of the *Blanche* then made it to shore, where they watched the total destruction of their ship and cargo and the burning of the English and Spanish flags.[2]

The Spaniards in Cuba, already displeased with the United States because of Lincoln's recent proclamation of slave emancipation, were enraged. Spanish officials and Cuban newspapers were indignant about what they deemed to be an insult to their honor. As soon as news of the incident reached the Captain General of Cuba, he dispatched Spanish warships from Havana to either capture or sink the *Montgomery*, but the Union warship had already gone to sea. The senior American naval officer in the area, arriving at Havana a week after the incident, met with the Captain General and denied knowledge of or having given sanction to the act, indicating that whoever committed it would be censured and that reparation would be made. Secretary of State Seward, upon hearing of the *Blanche* affair, wasted no time in instructing the new American minister to Spain, Gustave P. Koerner, to inform the Spanish government that the President had already organized an investigation and to assure that government that justice would be done.[3]

News of the *Blanche* affair reached Spain before Seward's message to Koerner arrived. The Spanish government ordered the immediate departure of five steam-driven warships to Cuba and directed a new forty-gun warship to follow within a week.[4] Fortunately, dexterous American diplomacy in Madrid smoothed potentially rough waters. The Spanish learned about the *Blanche* only hours before the new American minister was to be received by the Spanish queen. Spanish officials were at first inclined to postpone the reception, but changed their minds after being informed that such an act would be regarded as "a grave error" by the American government and would be "deeply regretted." The American chargé d'affaires assured the Spanish officials that his government was entirely unconnected with the *Blanche* outrage and would take the proper measures to reassure Spain of its good will. Negotiations between the Spanish and American officials in Madrid settled the question of remarks to be made at the reception by the queen and by Koerner about the *Blanche* affair, which could not be overlooked. Both speeches called for the renewal of good relations. Koerner's was especially warm and noted that nothing had happened with the knowledge or consent of the United States government to weaken Spanish-American relations. The queen regretted the events in Cuba, but she observed that Koerner's remarks had reassured her that the President of the United States would satisfy Spanish honor and rights and that relations between the two nations would remain unaltered.[5]

On October 20, Gabriel G. Tassara, the Spanish minister to Washington, addressed Seward on the subject of the

Blanche. Tassara described the affair and demanded satisfaction for a violation of Spanish territorial jurisdiction; for the insult to Spanish authority in the person of the sea *alcalde* and of his son, an insult aggravated by the capture of the Spanish pilot of the *Blanche;* for the insult to the Spanish and English flags, by "looking on them unmoved, and seeing them consumed" by flames; and for the burning of a neutral merchant vessel at Marianao as if the United States and Spain were at war with each other and without respect to existing treaties, declarations of the governments, or to international law. The Spanish minister insisted upon the immediate restoration of the pilot, a stop to measures such as were taken by the *Montgomery* in the interest of peace, and the censure of the American officer or officers involved in the case. Within a week, Seward promised an inquiry and all redress and satisfaction which might follow upon that inquiry, if justified, and Welles ordered the release of the pilot.[6]

On December 4 Tassara again complained to Seward, this time describing the affair as "an aggression suggested by a spirit of violence and of destructiveness which undervalues all rights, and displays the most complete forgetfulness of humanity." The Spaniard asked for the immediate dismissal of Commander Hunter of the *Montgomery* and for a trial so that he could suffer the consequences of his crimes. Tassara also demanded redress for the Spanish pilot and the English passenger taken aboard the *Montgomery*, who had since been released.[7]

Seward informed Tassara that Hunter would be immediately relieved of his command and tried by a court-martial. Hunter had acted in violation of instructions given to him and to all other American naval officers. His actions, direct violations of Spanish sovereignty and dignity, were therefore "regretted as well as disapproved and disavowed." Nevertheless, Seward continued, the Spanish pilot and the British traveler had leaped into one of the boats of the *Montgomery* to save themselves from the flames and had not been forced to go along with the Americans. The burning of ship and cargo, Seward concluded, was not a step taken by the Americans, but rather a deliberate act of the *Blanche's* captain.[8]

The British, like the Spanish, were angered by the *Blanche* incident. The English press was furious, and the law officers of the Crown considered the affair "to combine almost every circumstance of deliberate outrage upon the liberty and property of Her Majesty's subjects, and of insult to Her Majesty's flag" that could be imagined.[9]

Under instruction from Russell, Lord Lyons asked Seward for compensation on behalf of the British owners of the *Blanche* and her cargo and of the English subject "forcibly carried off" by the *Montgomery* and not released for several days. It also seemed that the same Englishman, a Mr. Robert Clement, was detained until he swore that the fire aboard the *Blanche* had been ignited by her own crew, a statement he later repudiated when no longer under duress. Clement, Lyons said, deserved an apology from the American government. Seward replied that an inquiry would be made into the facts.[10]

The trial of Commander Hunter took place in February 1862. The court charged Hunter with violating the territorial jurisdiction of Spain by taking possession of the *Blanche* in Spanish waters and with "scandalous conduct tending to the destruction of good morals," that is, extorting an oath from Clement. The court, relying only upon American testimony, found Hunter guilty of the first charge and innocent of the second. He was sentenced to be dismissed from the Navy. In spite of pleas by the court and by Welles in consideration of Hunter's zeal and good character, Lincoln saw to it that Hunter was dismissed from the service. Admiral David G. Farragut was convinced that Hunter had only done his duty with proper fervor, that legal questions should be left to the courts rather than to naval officers, and that Hunter had been sacrificed to maintain good relations with Spain—a curious attitude indeed for the presumably responsible commander of one of the Union blockading squadrons in the Gulf of Mexico. As late as 1922, Rear Admiral Albert Gleaves, writing in the *United States Naval Institute Proceedings,* drew from the *Blanche* affair the lesson that a naval officer should do what he thinks is right, even when it is legally wrong—"act boldly and take the chances." [11]

Seward had his final say on the case to Tassara in May, when he sent him his own analysis based upon the evidence submitted to him by the Spanish minister and by Welles. Seward observed that the steamer destroyed was in fact the *General Rusk,* an American vessel which had been seized by rebels and which had been renamed the *Blanche* in an attempt to defraud the United States, England, and Spain, and that the cargo was owned by Confederates. Hunter had indeed brought his vessel within Spanish waters and had dispatched boats to seize the *Rusk,* but the firing of the ship was not "committed, directed, authorized, foreseen or contemplated" by Hunter or by any of the officers or seamen of the *Montgomery*—it was the predetermined act of someone aboard the *Rusk,* the preparations for such a fire having been made at the port of embarkation under direction of the *Rusk's* captain.

The remonstrances of the *alcalde* and his son had been disregarded and threats may have been made to them, the Secretary of State continued, but this might be explained by the failure of the *Montgomery's* officers to understand Spanish. The son had been pushed, Seward admitted, but whether intentionally or not was uncertain. Nevertheless, the American officers and seamen must be held guilty of having been disrespectful of and defiant to the authority of Spain and its official agent. However, the *Montgomery's* officers and crew had not been disrespectful of the flags of England and Spain by watching them burn with indifference; their burning had been only an incident of the burning of the ship.

It also appeared to the Secretary of State that the Spanish pilot and Clement threw themselves into the American boats to escape the fire, and they had not been held under restraint. In addition, Clement's statement had been given voluntarily. Seward continued that the President disapproved of and regretted the entire proceeding of the violation of Spanish territory and all incidents of force or disrespect to the *alcalde* and his son and to the Spanish and British flags which may have occurred; but the Secretary of State denied that personal injuries or losses which occurred were due to the actions of the Americans, and he rejected claims of $311,859.29½. The State Department replaced the American Consul General at Havana, believed by the Spanish to have informed Hunter of the location of the *Blanche*, and the Navy Department promised to issue new instructions in order to prevent further violations of Spanish territory. Nevertheless, Spain received no pecuniary satisfaction.[12]

After Seward had rejected the Spanish claims for compensation, the British persisted on their own, insisting that the burning of the vessel and cargo, which they said were English, was the result of American "aggression." The English did not continue to insist on an apology for Clement after seeing Seward's final remarks to the Spanish. The Secretary of State, in response to the British, argued at different times that the *Blanche* was either American or Confederate, that the cargo was Confederate, and that the destruction of ship and cargo resulted from the actions of the ship's own crew. Hence, there could be no liability for the United States. Neither side gave in, and no compensation was ever paid.

Actually, the *Blanche* had been an American vessel seized by the Confederacy, then illegally transferred by an assistant quartermaster in the Confederate army to English friends who put her under the British flag. There was certainly considerable room for argument as to the legal ownership of the vessel —perhaps too much, for the case dropped from the diplomatic scene in 1866. The Mixed Commission on British and American Claims unanimously disallowed the claims of the British owner of the cargo several years later without giving any satisfactory explanation, thereby bringing the case to a close. The only satisfaction England ever received was an apology for any disrespect which may have appeared to have been shown towards the Union Jack.[13] But the *Blanche* affair was not the only problem that arose in Anglo-American relations from the violation of neutral territory.

The English government had fixed expectations for vessels of the Royal Navy and for belligerent warships in British waters. On January 18, 1862, the Admiralty instructed Vice-Admiral Milne, in command of Her Majesty's squadron in the North America and West India Station, not to interfere with belligerent operations beyond the three-mile limit off the shore of any British possession, but operations attempted within the limits of British territory should be prevented, by force if necessary. On January 31 Russell informed the Admiralty that warships of both belligerents were prohibited from departing from British territory within twenty-four hours after the departure of any vessel of the other belligerent; no warship of either belligerent could enter or remain in the Bahamas except by special permission or in case of stress of weather.[14]

The American Navy Department issued clear directions to Union vessels cruising near British waters. Welles ordered the commander of the West Gulf Blockading Squadron on August 8, 1862, for example, to guard closely the passages to Nassau, but he also cautioned the commander to conduct no hostile operations within a marine league of the coast of English possessions. In his orders to officers of August 18, 1862, the Secretary of the Navy insisted that "under no circumstances" were they to seize vessels within the waters of a friendly nation.[15] In spite of the instructions, a variety of problems involving the violation of neutral territory arose, mostly revolving around the activities of Acting Rear-Admiral Charles Wilkes.

On the suggestion of the President and the Secretary of State, Welles decided to organize a "flying squadron" in September 1862, under the command of Wilkes. Wilkes' primary job was to destroy Confederate cruisers in the West Indies and, secondarily, to seize vessels carrying contraband to the Confederacy. It was believed that the appointment of Wilkes would make the British more cautious in their activities, but it only aroused English hostility; the Nassau *Guardian* bemoaned the fact that the squadron was being placed under command of an officer "notorious for his precipitation, his contempt of law and usages, and for his deep dislike of England." Welles warned Wilkes to be inoffensive and to let no provocation induce him to invade the maritime jurisdiction of neutral powers, but the accusations began to fly soon after Wilkes arrived in the West Indies.[16]

Lyons informed Seward that Wilkes had revealed considerable ill feeling toward British officials in the West Indies. The British minister complained that Wilkes had been in effect blockading the port of Bermuda; that he had maintained a system of cruising in Bermuda waters in violation of international law; that he had placed sentinels on British territory; and that when the Governor of Bermuda "instructed" (in the sense of "informed") Wilkes that his ship could not be permitted to return to Bermuda because a belligerent vessel coaling in a British port could not return there for three months, Wilkes replied that the American government alone had the power to instruct him. When questioned, Wilkes informed

Welles that his vessels had only cruised outside of Bermuda waters; that the only sentinels he had placed ashore were on a wharf to prevent liquor from being smuggled aboard his ships; and that he had courteously informed the government about who could instruct an American officer. Welles and Seward defended Wilkes even before the arrival of Wilkes' own defense. Seward informed Lyons that Wilkes had and would continue to act courteously and in conformity with international law when dealing with the British. At the same time, Welles advised Wilkes that while he should be vigilant, he should also give heed to neutral rights and avoid so far as possible visiting English ports, where the colonial authorities sympathized so obviously with the rebels.[17]

Wilkes departed from Bermuda in early October 1862, but he left two warships behind just outside of English jurisdiction, and they successfully intimidated would-be blockade-runners for two more weeks. Wilkes himself was soon at Nassau. When he was told by a Nassau pilot that his warship could not be anchored without the permission of the governor of the Bahamas, Wilkes replied that he would anchor "whether the Governor like it or no." In order to avoid an official refusal, however, Wilkes would not allow an officer of the British warship *Barracouta* to board his vessel. G. J. Malcolm, commander of the *Barracouta*, called on the American consul at Nassau and asked the consul to inform Wilkes that he was anchored in British waters and that if he remained there after official warning, the *Barracouta* would fire on his flagship. Fortunately the matter was resolved without incident; Vice-Admiral Milne reprimanded Malcolm for his statement to the consul, and Seward told Lyons that new orders had been issued to naval commanders to respect scrupulously the rights and regulations of neutrals. Both Seward and Lyons promised that the naval officers of America and England would treat each other with the utmost courtesy.[18]

Wilkes was also determined to end the use of the harbor of St. Thomas in the Danish West Indies as a rendezvous and jumping-off point for blockade-runners, and he again got himself into trouble, this time with both the Danish and English governments. In early April 1863, Lieutenant-Governor Louis Rothe of St. Thomas wrote Wilkes, suggesting that he take steps to prevent American men-of-war in Danish waters from "preparing and commencing the persecution, overhauling, and capture of any vessel" admitted to free commercial intercourse at St. Thomas. Wilkes denied that such activities had been taking place—"The idea of our using your harbor to make preparations or of infringing upon your neutral territory has never been conceived." [19]

The Danes did not find Wilkes' remarks entirely convincing and turned to the State Department. The Danish government complained that American warships were using the port of St. Thomas as a station for watching and lying in wait for neutral merchant ships which were later stopped and captured outside of that port. Although the *Peterhoff* and the *Dolphin* had been seized outside of Danish territory, constituting no violation of Danish sovereignty, the continuing use of St. Thomas as a base might seriously affect the favorable attitude of the Danish government toward the United States during the war. The Danes asked Welles for assurances which might relieve their apprehensions.[20]

Welles believed that Wilkes and other American naval officers had scrupulously observed the rights of neutrals and that Wilkes' professions to Rothe should be adequate assurance. Because of Denmark's involvement in the Schleswig–Holstein issue and the fact that Wilkes was soon recalled, no further correspondence took place on the subject between the United States and Denmark.[21] England was not placated, however, since she was generally the one hurt by

Wilkes alleged procedures at St. Thomas. The *Peterhoff* and *Dolphin* cases supported this point.

In November of 1862 the U.S.S. *Tuscarora* had seized the British merchantman *Thistle* off Madeira. At that time Lyons had informed Seward that it was illegal for American cruisers to make belligerent use of a neutral port, and that "a more un-neutral use of a port could not be well conceived than lying in wait in it for the vessels of another neutral state, as they entered and left it, and, on their passing the limits of three miles, boarding and visiting them, and then returning to the port." Seward had replied that the American commander involved would be censured if the case was as described. On May 4, 1863, Lyons reminded Seward of the case and of the British government's response to the seizure. On May 7 Lyons said that another American warship, the U.S.S. *Wachusetts*, was making use of St. Thomas as a place from which to capture vessels of neutral states as they passed the three-mile limit and that Her Majesty's government regarded this as "a very grave offense, and as a gross abuse of the power of a belligerent." Lyons told Seward confidentially that Milne had expressed his apprehension that if American naval officers persisted as they had been, serious complications would arise, responsibility for which would rest upon the American government.[22]

Lyons wrote Russell on May 11 that the two things that he was most anxious to obtain immediately were the removal of Wilkes from the West Indies and the withdrawal of the American squadron from St. Thomas. He was cautious about both goals, saying nothing to Seward about the latter one, and was particularly concerned that he should not appear to have anything to do with the removal of Wilkes. Seward assured Lyons that Wilkes would soon be transferred to the Pacific. On June 1 Wilkes was recalled from duty in the West Indies, the result primarily of the persistent complaints of neutral powers against his allegedly illicit and arrogant acts. The recall was also due to Wilkes' detention of the U.S.S. *Vanderbilt* in violation of orders and his failure in his main mission, the capture of Confederate cruisers. England breathed easier once Wilkes was removed.[23]

Welles instructed the new commander of the West India Squadron fully on what his behavior should be toward neutrals. Neutral ports should not be visited if it could be avoided; when they were visited, all established regulations must be respected. Friendly relations between American naval officers and those of other powers, especially of England, should be cultivated. The waters of neutral nations must not be trespassed, and Welles spelled out clearly that it was illegal to chase, fire upon, bring to, or capture any vessel within neutral waters, or to use neutral territory as a base for following and seizing any vessel.[24] In a word, Wilkes' transgressions were not to be repeated.

Unaware of these instructions, Lyons demanded assurances that the American navy would not persist in behaving as it had at St. Thomas. Seward passed the British communication on to Welles, who replied that although the appropriate instructions had been issued, the Navy Department could not be expected to instruct its officers completely on matters such as the rights of neutrals on which the most learned lawyers and the highest courts might differ in opinion. Seward, however, told Lyons that Wilkes' replacement had been properly instructed. Although the British government still suspected that the *Peterhoff* and the *Dolphin* had been pursued in violation of Danish neutrality, they felt there was nothing they could do so long as the Danish government was satisfied with the American explanations. In any event, the appropriate orders had been given.[25]

Another territorial violation had taken place at the end of

December 1862, when one of Wilkes' officers, Commander Napoleon Collins, seized the English schooner *Mont Blanc* at the south end of Great Bahama Island within a league of the shore. The district court at Key West released the ship because it had been taken in British waters, but no costs were granted because there appeared to have been probable cause for capture. Lyons insisted on compensation for the owners, protested the violation of English territory, and requested renewed instructions to naval officers to prevent a repetition of such activities. Seward and the President agreed that compensation was in order, admitted the violation of English territory, and promised the issuance of renewed instructions to officers. Welles reluctantly informed Commander Collins that he had incurred the displeasure of the President by his action and that a repetition of such proceedings would call forth more severe censure.[26]

According to Collins, Wilkes had told him that he could make captures within a league of uninhabited cays and inlets, as was the case when he took the *Mont Blanc*. Welles immediately wrote Seward that since the court had found probable cause for the seizure, the censure of Collins should be removed. Seward pointed out that the prize court had admitted to a violation of neutral territory and that Lincoln was of opinion that the censure could not be withdrawn without giving offense to the English government. In spite of Welles' efforts to obstruct the granting of compensation to the owners of the *Mont Blanc* for detention of their vessel, they were paid in the summer of 1864. Welles was bitter; he was convinced that Seward's fear that an American naval officer would precipitate a war with England enabled Lyons to take advantage of Seward, "who in his fears yields everything almost before it is asked." Although Lincoln and Seward had in fact determined to avoid difficulties with England in this case, they had ample justification for giving in to English demands, especially since the negotiations over the *Mont Blanc* case paralleled those concerning other alleged violations of neutral territory and since there was intense foreign pressure on the Union government to prevent such practices.[27]

Yet another case of alleged violation of neutral territory occurred on May 30, 1863, when the U.S.S. *Rhode Island*, commanded by Stephen D. Trenchard, forced the Confederate steamer *Margaret and Jessie* ashore on the island of Eleuthera, a British possession in the Bahamas. According to the evidence submitted to Lord Russell by the Confederate commissioner in London, the *Rhode Island* chased the rebel ship into British waters, and fired upon her until she was disabled and run ashore. The *Rhode Island* came so close to shore that a number of her shells struck Eleuthera Island, cutting trees and ploughing up the soil. The British press described the incident as a "ferocious outrage," indicative of "lawless and brutal indifference to law and human life." The *Army and Navy Gazette* asked, "If at Eleuthera, why not at the Isle of Wight, in Southampton Water?" The newspapers pressed the English government to act, and act it did, demanding explanations and redress.[28]

The Navy Department ordered a court of inquiry to be held at the Boston Navy Yard. The court found that Commander Trenchard had been careful not to violate British territorial jurisdiction and had cautioned his pilot to avoid taking the *Rhode Island* nearer than four or five miles from shore; the pilot was to inform Trenchard if that distance was reached or if the chase should get within three miles of land. The pilot failed to so inform Trenchard, but the court was certain that the Union warship was never closer than four miles from shore. The court concluded, therefore, that Trenchard had been anxious to avoid any violation of English territorial jurisdiction and had not made such a violation while chasing the *Margaret and Jessie*.[29]

The law officers of the Crown felt that the court had been justified in coming to that conclusion on the basis of the evidence before them. The officers assumed that no testimony had been given by the crew of the *Margaret and Jessie* because they were enemies of the United States, but that such evidence and the testimony of passengers aboard the rebel steamer might have led the court to another conclusion. They believed, however, that the *Rhode Island* could well have been over three miles from shore since the Parrot gun aboard her was said to be able to fire shells a distance of five miles, which would explain the presence of shell fragments on shore. Nevertheless, shells from the American vessel did damage trees and endanger lives on Eleuthera. The law officers felt that neutral lives and property should not be exposed to such dangers, no matter from what distance the shells were fired. Although they were certain there had been no intent to violate British jurisdiction, such a violation might have occurred inadvertently as a result of an incorrect impression of the distance to shore. This view was presented to Seward, along with the expression of hope that the United States government would agree with the British that warships should not fire guns from any distance which would permit shells to fall in neutral waters or territory.[30]

The *Margaret and Jessie* incident brought to the surface a question which had been only quietly and occasionally discussed during the war, that of extending the territorial jurisdiction of national waters beyond the traditional three mile limit in order to prevent violations of neutral territory. In October 1862, Spain had claimed that her jurisdiction extended six miles from the coast of Cuba. Welles had strongly opposed acknowledging that claim as it could only aid blockade-runners chased by American cruisers by giving them a greater area for refuge. In addition, such a novel interpretation of international law was being proposed at a rather inopportune

time for the United States. The State Department informed
the Spanish of this view, adding that the question was not one
which Spain could decide unilaterally.[31]

When the British expressed concern about the shells of
belligerents falling into neutral territory, Seward realized that
the extent of neutral jurisdiction was again in question. The
French had also expressed concern that belligerent shells
might fall on their soil. The State Department held that the
discussion of the extension of neutral jurisdiction resulting
from improvements in artillery was not out of place, but it
did feel that the United States was entitled to the advantage
of the existing law for the duration of her civil war and that
any new interpretation of the law should be agreed upon by
the principal maritime powers.[32]

The British government gave serious thought to the matter. The Admiralty concluded that the present law was adequate: no serious inconvenience had resulted from belligerent
shells falling within neutral waters; violations of neutral territory would be increased if the limits of a nation's jurisdiction
were extended; such extension would give additional immunity from capture to slavers; extended asylum would be
claimed by enemy ships in case of war with England; and
such extension might mean exclusion of British fishermen
from working within an enlarged distance from the French
and other coasts. The Privy Council for Trade concurred in
this view, stressing that the extension of territorial jurisdiction
could only aid an enemy by granting additional facilities for
refuge and would therefore lessen England's advantage of possessing the world's most powerful navy. The law officers
agreed with the foregoing views and, since no serious incidents occurred subsequent to that of the *Margaret and Jessie*,
the whole question disappeared for the remainder of the
war.[33]

The numerous violations of neutral territory by American naval officers had been disapproved by their government, though not to any great extent. The Navy Department issued renewed and expanded instructions after unhappy diplomatic encounters, but violations continued to take place even after the *Margaret and Jessie* incident. The State Department invariably made the minimum gestures to pacify indignant neutrals.

Captain Hunter had been dismissed from the Navy because he had violated his orders and jeopardized American relations with Spain, even creating a situation in which Spanish warships were sent out with instructions to seize or sink his ship. Welles, Farragut, the court which tried Hunter, and an American rear admiral writing in an American naval journal sixty years after the *Blanche* affair all would have exonerated Hunter on the basis of his patriotic zeal; but the President and the Secretary of State recognized the lack of an alternative to the dismissal of Hunter from the Navy—statesmanship came first. The State Department apologized for the violation of Spanish territory, but refused to admit American guilt for the burning of the *Blanche*, although the ship's destruction certainly would not have occurred had not the *Montgomery* chased her into Spanish waters. All in all, the State Department handled the *Blanche* incident fairly well, although the fact that no war between Spain and the United States erupted should probably be attributed in the first instance to the chance inability of the Spanish warships to locate the *Montgomery*.

The other violations of neutral territory in no way improved American relations with foreign nations. The appointment of Charles Wilkes to the command of the West India Squadron, after his involvement in the *Trent* affair, must be regarded as a blunder of substantial magnitude; he antagonized nearly everyone with whom he came in contact—and this finally included the Secretary of the Navy. During the last months of 1862 and the first five months of 1863, Wilkes managed to seriously exacerbate relations with England and even to draw a negative response from Denmark, the one nation which was consistently friendly to the United States during the war. Finally, under indirect pressure from Lyons and direct pressure from Seward, Welles removed Wilkes from his command and issued comprehensive directions to his replacement to the effect that Wilkes' errors should not be repeated.

Again overriding the wishes of the Navy Department, Lincoln and Seward saw to it that Commander Collins was censured and that compensation was paid as a consequence of the seizure of the *Mont Blanc* in English waters. The Navy Department inquiry exonerated Commander Trenchard from violating neutral territory when chasing the *Margaret and Jessie,* but the British government had its doubts. The diplomatic pressure was so intense, and the President and the Secretary of State stated so clearly the necessity of avoiding any further infringements of neutral territory, that Gideon Welles and his officers apparently understood at last, and no more serious incidents occurred. Statesmanship finally triumphed over naval zeal.

8

The *Emily St. Pierre:*
One That Got Away

LIVERPOOL, England, in the spring of 1862 could not have been considered friendly toward the Union cause in the Civil War. Although shopkeepers, artisans, and workers sympathized with the North, government leaders and the upper classes supported the South. The United States consul in Liverpool, Thomas H. Dudley, was convinced that pro-Confederate Englishmen were motivated by desire for commercial supremacy and profit. By constructing a navy for the South, they would help sweep Northern commerce from the seas; and Liverpool was one of the centers of English shipbuilding. In addition, large profits would accrue from supplying the South with arms, munitions, and supplies. The cotton trade was predominant in Liverpool, and a tariff-free South could only be a joy to cloth manufacturers. Consul Dudley often received threatening letters and was subjected to social snubs and sneers. The flag of the American consulate, for example, was often found with kettles and bricks tied to it as a sign of contempt.[1]

When the English ship *Emily St. Pierre* sailed up to the docks of her home port at Liverpool one day in 1861, flying the palmetto flag of South Carolina, she created a sensation. On April 21, 1862, she again arrived at Liverpool, this time having aboard as prisoners the Union prize crew which had unsuccessfully endeavored to take the vessel to a Union port for adjudication. Once more, the applause was spirited.[2]

Dudley telegraphed Charles Francis Adams to inform him of the most recent exploit of the *Emily St. Pierre* and to ask for instructions. The news of the "rescue," the legal term for the type of recapture described, caused Adams more grief than he had felt over any other news he had received in months. The Undersecretary of the American legation considered the rescue to be "mortifying in conscience" and "verily heart-sickening." Adams directed Dudley to take the depositions of the Union sailors, who had been released, and he made plans for claiming the vessel. The depositions of the prize crew, the description of events given by the captain and the steward of the *St. Pierre*, and the Union report on the initial capture enable us to reconstruct the story.[3]

On November 27, 1861, the *Emily St. Pierre*, under Captain William Wilson, put to sea from Calcutta, India. Her cargo consisted of 2,173 bales of gunny cloth. According to Wilson's report, the vessel was to make for the coast of South Carolina, ascertain whether the Civil War was over and, if it was, take on a pilot and enter the port of Charleston. If the harbor was blockaded, Wilson was to proceed to St. John, New Brunswick. On March 18, 1862, the ship was taken by the Union blockaders three and a half miles off Charleston as she headed straight for the bar. The captors had her name on the blacklist. They suspected that she had contraband on board and that her papers were fraudulent, her destination in fact being Charleston and not St. John. It seemed likely to the Union officers that the vessel was owned by the Charleston firm of Fraser and Co., not by citizens of a neutral nation. In addition, the ship had been seen flying the Confederate banner only fifteen days before leaving Calcutta. She was therefore thought to be Confederate property. The Union commander ordered the vessel to Philadelphia for adjudication under charge of Acting Master Josiah Stone and a prize crew. Captain Wilson, his steward, and the cook of the *St. Pierre* were kept aboard the vessel so that they could be questioned by the prize court.[4]

About thirty miles off Cape Hatteras, North Carolina, Wilson came on deck and spoke pleasantly to Stone of the fair wind blowing during the night. A few minutes later he asked Stone to accompany him into the cabin to indicate the ship's position on the chart. Stone was willing and the two men went inside. As Stone bent over the chart, Wilson grabbed the prize master by the collar, drew forth a belaying pin from under his vest, and threatened Stone's life. At the same moment, the cook and steward sprang out of hiding armed with revolvers which, Stone later observed, "they presented at my head, and the captain called out for them to blow my brains out, saying, 'You damned pirates come on board my ship to take her!'" Stone said he was no pirate and pleaded with the men to spare his life. He was then put in irons and locked in a room, later being informed by Wilson that he was at liberty to take passage to England. Within an hour after Stone was taken, the captain, steward, and cook recaptured the ship from the fourteen remaining members of the prize crew.

Only one mishap occurred: a member of the prize crew was shot through the shoulder when he went for the steward with a knife. By bribes and threats, four members of the prize crew were persuaded to work the ship to England. One month later, the *Emily St. Pierre* arrived triumphantly in Liverpool.[5]

Wilson was given recognition for the rescue of the *St. Pierre* in a testimonial presented at the Liverpool Mercantile Marine Association and in the form of gifts from 170 Liverpool merchants, although the rescue was due primarily to the loyalty of the steward, Mr. Mathew Montgomery, to the former captain and part owner of the vessel; and Montgomery admittedly hoped for "some advantage" for himself. The steward had had little difficulty in persuading the cook to join with him, but Captain Wilson cooperated only with reluctance—though he would later claim all the credit.[6]

The case is significant in a number of ways. First, the usual positions of the United States and Great Britain with regard to prize cases during the Civil War were reversed. This time America would play the role of injured party and make claims against England. In addition, recaptures by neutral crews of vessels suspected of being involved in illegal trade were rare. Neutrals were not generally treated as prisoners of war when taken aboard seized vessels; most members of a captured crew were immediately released, while a handful of men were detained only temporarily in order to testify before the prize court. Once they had testified, they were free to go. The *St. Pierre* case would cause Union naval officers to fear the recurrence of similar incidents and to treat neutral subjects with severity.[7]

Secretary of the Navy Welles was quite displeased when he received news of the recapture of the *St. Pierre*, for he had recently given instructions to commanders of blockading squadrons urging humane treatment and discouraging the use of irons for captured neutral crews. He received a bitter letter from Samuel F. Du Pont, commander of the South Atlantic Blockading Squadron, who blamed the recapture on the orders issued by the Navy Department for lenient treatment of neutrals. Du Pont expressed the hope that the government would insist upon the return of the *St. Pierre* to United States courts for adjudication, inasmuch as rescue by the crew of a neutral vessel was, he believed, illegal. Welles hastened to inform Secretary of State Seward of Du Pont's and his own views on the subject. But the Navy had little to worry about with respect to the Department of State. Charles Francis Adams had acted promptly upon receipt of the depositions taken by Dudley, and his actions were just as quickly approved by Seward.[8]

On April 24 Adams had written to Lord Russell, informing him of the case. Adams observed that Wilson's behavior required, according to international law, confiscation of vessel and cargo by the United States, for his act strongly indicated the unlawful intent of the voyage. The American representative trusted that Russell would early consider the restoration of the vessel to authorities of the United States.[9]

After consulting the law officers of the Crown, Russell replied that the British government had no legal power to interfere with the property of English citizens. Recapture of an English vessel by a neutral, Russell continued, however punishable as a violation against international law in the prize courts of the belligerent administering such law, was no offense against the municipal law of England.[10]

In his rejoinder to Russell, the American minister observed that Lord Stowell, the highest English judicial authority, had laid down the law applicable to the present case in most precise terms. Adams quoted Stowell in language similar to that in his first letter to Russell. He then commented that, as far as he could determine, Russell was declining to act on behalf of the United States not on the basis of the merits of the case, but for reasons "purely technical." Yet, if he needed justification to act, Russell had only to look at the Queen's neutrality proclamation of May 13, 1861. The last paragraph of that document warned that British subjects who acted in contempt of British neutrality, in violation of the law of nations, would suffer the penal consequences of municipal or international law. If Adams had misinterpreted the proclamation, then surely it had been "most unfortunately worded." [11]

Russell retorted that the decision of Lord Stowell to which Adams referred was applicable to the *Emily St. Pierre* case, but not quite in the way Adams viewed it. An American prize court might have legally condemned the vessel if the attempted rescue had failed and if the ship had been brought within the jurisdiction of such a court. But the judgment of Lord Stowell furnished no authority for contending that the municipal law of a neutral country was under any obligation or had any jurisdiction to enforce or aid in enforcing the rights of the belligerent to capture. Far from declining to comply with Adams' request on a purely technical basis, Russell insisted that he was acting in strict accord with a primary principle of international law which stated that a neutral had no right to inquire into the validity of a capture unless the rights of neutrals had been violated. Not only was Adams' request without foundation in international law, it was not even supported by the doctrine and practice of the United States government.

Adams had in fact misunderstood the neutrality proclamation. It stated that any breach of the proclamation would be punished by English law, while any breach of international law, not also a breach of the statute, would be left to the determination of the courts entitled to enforce that law. Unless an American court found that the vessel had violated international law dealing with the duties of neutrals—at the same time violating the portions of the Foreign Enlistment Act which were enumerated in the proclamation—then the title to neutral property could not be transferred to the captor. The British government, therefore, would not depart from its earlier decision given in answer to Adams' demand.[12]

Two days after receipt of this message, Adams made an interesting notation in his diary: "In answer to my long series of complaints *based on serious grounds of dissatisfaction though perhaps not permissible on technical grounds*, I can not recollect a single instance in which there has been the slightest indication of disapproval whatever of the action [taken by the captain, steward, and cook of the *Emily St. Pierre*] . . . however notoriously fraudulent." [italics added] [13] Adams was thus admitting that he had no valid legal claim on England, but that he was merely displeased with the British attitude toward the case. In effect, he hoped that the English government would help the United States enforce its blockade of the Southern coast. Russell's interpretation of neutral duties was the correct one, for had England in any way aided the Northern blockade, she would have abandoned a position of neutrality. Adams' view indicates a sense of futility and perhaps also a naiveté which impelled him to clutch at legalistic straws.

Though dubious of the reception which might be accorded another reply, Adams wrote again to Russell. He noted that Lord Stowell stated clearly that even instructions from owners would not justify a ship in coming to the mouth of a blockaded port for inquiry. The *St. Pierre*, Adams continued, subjected herself to strong suspicion of a fraudulent endeavor to break the blockade. International law presumed that a captain and crew, seized on this basis, were innocent until proven otherwise. The law of nations therefore dictated the most lenient treatment of such neutrals. But when a captain resorted to force against the lawful agents of a belligerent government, he committed a hostile and illegal act, subjecting himself to imprisonment and his vessel and cargo to confiscation as if they were enemy property.

As far as Adams was concerned, the obligation to inflict the penalty did not belong exclusively to the injured nation, but belonged instead to those whose subjects were "wicked enough to commit the wrong." [14] If neutral crews were allowed to use violence to escape a legal inquiry with impunity, then the detention of neutral ships would become "a scene of mutual hostility and contention; the crews of neutral ships must be guarded with all the severity and strictness practised upon actual prisoners of war, for the same measures of precaution and distrust will become equally necessary." Since the British government preferred to leave the judgment of violations of international law to the courts of the United States, a person was considered an offender only if he was caught by a Union warship while committing an offense. If only one power could seize and judge international lawbreakers, there was no need for peace treaties or alliances between nations. If a government was not prepared to prevent or to rectify acts of violence by its own subjects, then it could hardly complain if the punishment awarded by foreign nations should happen, unavoidably at times, to involve the innocent and the guilty in a common fate.[15]

After appealing to the sanctity of international law and threatening harsh treatment of neutrals, Adams called Russell's attention to the *Trent* affair. The American government had released the two Confederate commissioners to Europe seized aboard the British mail packet without reference to municipal law, but because their seizure seemed to have been illegal according to international law. The United States government had not pleaded that it lacked the power to relinquish the Confederate statesmen. And the British government would hardly have accepted the argument that the courts of Great Britain were the only tribunals competent to enforce the penalties for commission of wrong.[16]

Russell's reply ignored both the "spirit" of international law and Adams' threats. The rescue of the *Emily St. Pierre*, Russell observed, was an act in violation of the rights accruing to a belligerent under the law of nations; that law permitted only the belligerent to defend his rights. The same law neither required nor permitted neutral nations to carry out belligerent rights.

In answer to Adams' reference to the *Trent* affair, Russell noted that the flagrant wrong was done by a United States naval officer. The prisoners, whose release was demanded, were in the direct custody of the Executive Department; the United States government had the power to free them, which it did. The *St. Pierre* was not in the hands of the English government, and both English municipal law and the law of nations forbade the British government from taking that ship away from its legal owners.[17] Russell might also have added that had the United States refused to release the Confederate commissioners taken from the *Trent*, England might have declared war. In the case of the *St. Pierre*, the United States was in no position to threaten England with hostilities.

Adams answered that he had had enough of a futile correspondence and indicated that, as far as he was concerned, his note would complete the discussion of the subject. The same day he replied to Russell, Adams wrote Seward that it seemed apparent that the only remaining recourse was, in case of seizures, to put the seized neutral officers in irons.[18] Fortunately for Anglo-American relations, his recommendation was not adopted.

Part of the explanation for this rejection might be found in the response of the British Foreign Office to a memorial, presented by a number of Liverpool merchants and shipowners, pleading the necessity of protection for British shipping against repeated seizures by Federal cruisers. Austen H. Layard, Undersecretary of State for Foreign Affairs, first pointed out to these petitioners the arguments made by the Americans against the actions of British traders and shippers, and then observed that Lord Russell wished neither to confirm nor deny the truth of the American allegations.

The British government had, Layard continued, done everything that it reasonably could to prevent violations of neutral rights: it had urged the Federal government to direct its naval officers to act with greater caution in the exercise of their belligerent rights, and it had intervened on behalf of British subjects in every case in which it was justified in so doing. There was, however, only one practical solution: merchants and shipowners should avoid illicit trade. That trade exposed innocent commerce to vexatious detention and search by American cruisers: it produced irritation and ill-will on the part of the Americans; it was contrary to the spirit of the British neutrality proclamation; and it exposed the British name to suspicions of bad faith, of which neither the British government nor the mass of the people were guilty.[19]

Layard's answer was no doubt intended to mollify the American government. As early as March of 1862, Seward and Adams had pressed the British government to do something to restrain British subjects trading with the Confederacy. Layard's communication, dated July 5, 1862, revealed the farthest deviation from strict neutrality that the English government to date was willing to admit, but it was at least a gesture toward improving Anglo-American relations.

In a confidential message, Lord Russell informed Adams of his government's reply to the memorial. When the news reached Washington, Lincoln and Seward regarded it with much satisfaction. The British government may have been prompted to act as it did by an indication of good will made by Minister Adams a few weeks earlier. Six weeks before the Layard memorial was issued and four days after Adams sent his concluding letter on the *Emily St. Pierre* to Russell, the Undersecretary of the American legation in London, Benjamin Moran, happened upon a curious correspondence in some early volumes of the *American State Papers*. He discovered that several rescues, almost identical to that of the *St. Pierre*, had been effected in 1799. In those cases, the British government had made claims on almost the selfsame grounds taken by Adams, and the Americans had declined to accede to them for substantially the same reasons given by Lord Russell. On May 3, 1800, Secretary of State Timothy Pickering had written the British minister in Washington, Robert Liston, that he was unaware of any precedent for returning a rescued ship and cargo to belligerent authorities, "nor does any reason occur which should require the neutral to exert its power in aid of the right of the belligerent nation in such captures." [20]

Sixty-two years later, Minister Adams, on his own responsibility, reluctantly called Russell's attention to the precedent. Russell received the information with great delight. The British Foreign Secretary announced the discovery in the House of Commons, and praised Adams and his grandfather, John Adams, who had been President in 1800 when the early decision had been made. The American minister was pleased by Russell's kind words, and the case of the *Emily St. Pierre* was at last closed.[21]

The citing of precedents in matters of international law, as in the *St. Pierre* case, revealed itself to be a double-edged blade. Lord Russell's argument, opposing the restoration of the *St. Pierre*, had been at an earlier time employed by the United States against England; it was now used by England against the United States. On the other hand, the United States revived the doctrine of continuous voyage, formerly used by England against American shipping, and now used it as a weapon against British commerce.

The rescue of the *St. Pierre* raised the question of the proper treatment by a belligerent of a neutral seized aboard a suspected blockade-runner. This problem was a constant source of irritation in Anglo-American relations throughout the Civil War. England favored a lenient treatment of the neutrals involved and had the law of nations on her side. Union naval officers, having been enlightened by cases such as the *Emily St. Pierre* and impressed with the pro-Confederate nature of the trade in which neutrals were engaged, occasionally treated captured neutrals virtually as prisoners of war.

9

The Treatment of
Neutral Subjects

In their determination to do their duty, Union naval officers at times seriously mistreated neutral subjects taken aboard suspected vessels. They did so despite the convention of international law which permitted a belligerent to detain neutrals only briefly as witnesses before a prize court and which forbade their treatment as prisoners of war. Neutrals whose nationality was in question, suspected of being Union or Confederate citizens, and neutrals who persisted in running the blockade, were placed in Northern jails and military prisons where they were sometimes treated as prisoners of war. Some neutrals were required to swear not to engage in blockade-running in the future. Although England repeatedly condemned such incidents, the United States resisted British pressure, further straining Anglo-American relations.

The British government made its position clear in 1861, though only a few incidents occurred that year. Four crew members of the *Revere* and the *Louisa Agnes*, British vessels seized for violation of blockade, were temporarily placed in irons by a prize crew from the capturing Union warship. The alleged purpose of this act was to prevent those so confined from rescuing their ship. Vice-Admiral Milne emphasized to Lyons that the coercion of unresisting crews from seized neutral vessels was a direct violation of international law and that it was highly unlikely that the men involved in the cases had either the desire or the power to rescue their vessel. Crews of such vessels must not be considered prisoners of war. Lyons pressed the case on Seward, who in turn persuaded Welles to issue instructions that naval officers should not maltreat captured neutrals and should use irons only if the safety of captors and prizes was threatened. Prisoners taken from two other vessels seized later in 1861 were released as soon as it was learned they were neutral subjects.[1]

Neutral blockade-runners went relatively unscathed at first, but their treatment became increasingly harsh. In March 1862 William Jones Fisher, a crew-member of the just-captured English schooner *Telegraph*, was kept in handcuffs aboard a Union warship for three days and nights. The prize master had ordered the *Telegraph's* sails furled. Fisher, who was drunk at the time, cursed the prize officers and informed them that if they wanted the sails furled, they could do the job themselves. The captain of the ship refused to stop Fisher's abusive language. Fisher was then handcuffed and removed in order to restrain him from committing violence en route to port.

Lord Lyons complained to Seward that the imprisonment of Fisher was "an unjustifiable act of violence and cruelty" and that England would not acquiesce in the treatment of British subjects "with ignominy." Seward's reply noted the necessity of restraining Fisher to prevent him from either attempting to rescue his ship or endangering the lives of the captors. The conclusion drawn from the *Emily St. Pierre* case, Seward remarked, seemed to be that a belligerent must rely upon his own strength to prevent rescues. Neither Seward nor Lord Lyons would budge, and the case ended in a stalemate.[2]

A few months later the British stated that a neutral subject caught while involved in blockade-running could not be lawfully punished or exposed to personal ill-treatment. According to the officers and crew of the blockade-runner *Mersey*, their maltreatment violated accepted principles of law. The British protested the alleged confinement of the *Mersey's* officers and crew as prisoners of war, the robbery of their private effects, and the efforts made to prevent some members of the crew from giving evidence. Gideon Welles proved that all of the charges were false, and England accepted his decision.[3]

The *Mersey* case was not the only one in which captured blockade-runners distorted facts. The British charged the captors of the *Emilie* with being intoxicated, jumping upon the Union Jack, and looting and destroying property aboard the prize—allegations based upon the statements of the blockade-runners. The charges, like those against the *Mersey*, were refuted. British seamen released by the Union government subsequent to their capture aboard the *Sunbeam* complained that "every inducement" had been held out to persuade them to join the Northern army or navy—measures England considered inconsistent with the obligations of a belligerent towards a neutral government. Yet the English did not press their case when Seward pointed out that "every inducement" did not include duress, force, menace, bribery, or deceitful representations. One of the law officers of the Crown subsequently warned Lord Russell to be wary of the statements of blockade-runners; Lord Lyons, after more such encounters, wrote Russell privately: "I do not know whether the captors ever tell the truth . . . the captured *never* do." [4] Nevertheless, there would be ample reason to complain.

The question of oaths for foreigners engaged in block-ade-running first arose in January 1862. Three crew-members of the recently captured *Adeline* were released after being made to swear not to be again employed in a similar opera-tion. Under pressure from Lyons, Seward informed Welles that such oaths were illegal. Welles then directed his officers to consider the men released under oath to be absolved from their obligation and to make no similar exactions in the future. [5]

Major-General Benjamin F. Butler, who commanded the Department of the Gulf, was concerned with neutral subjects running the blockade, furnishing arms and munitions of war, and in other ways aiding the Confederates. Early in June of 1862, he ordered that neutrals resident in his department take an oath to the effect that they could not "act or consent that any be done, or conceal any that has been or is about to be done, that shall aid or comfort any of the enemies . . . of the United States whatever." The consuls of seven foreign nations in New Orleans immediately protested the required oath be-cause it was inconsistent with the neutrality of their subjects. The British made clear their opposition to the oath. [6]

Butler, later recalled partly for his inability to get along with foreign representatives, merely insulted the consuls. Sew-ard, on the other hand, had the required oath nullified. But-ler received a personal message from General-in-Chief Henry W. Halleck: "Oaths are not to be prescribed by us to aliens." Nevertheless, Seward would reverse himself in 1863, and Englishmen would on occasion have to give oath in order to gain release from detention—the English government be damned. [7] Here again was an undoubtedly ad hoc approach. Yet perhaps it had a design: if neutral subjects could be kept in a state of uncertainty about American rules, possibly they would be less inclined to violate the blockade.

By the end of 1862 Lyons had made some progress in preventing the mistreatment of British subjects. Although he had few cases which provided substance for strong and sustained complaints, Lyons was able to persuade the Union government to order the release of foreign subjects not needed as witnesses and to abandon the oath requirement for foreigners. The general orders for the Union navy issued on January 1, 1863, reiterated what Lyons had pressed for and secured in 1861—the stipulation that captured neutrals would be treated with kindness, and that irons would only be used when absolutely necessary for the safety of captors and prizes.[8] Whether the directions on paper would always be practiced was another matter.

One of the more serious cases concerning the abuse of a neutral occurred in 1863; it involved the fireman of the prize ship *Nicolai I*, James O'Neill, who was severely wounded by an American officer, temporarily placed in irons, and imprisoned without any reasonable justification for over half a year. According to O'Neill, his ship was taken on March 21 by Acting Master Alfred Everson of the U.S.S. *Victoria* off Wilmington. O'Neill agreed to continue working as fireman aboard the prize until it reached New York. While showing a prize officer the layout of the *Nicolai's* machinery, O'Neill mentioned that large quantities of gunpowder were stored nearby. Both men agreed that it would be a good idea to place a sentry below to prevent any of the prize crew from smoking in the area or being careless with lights. The officer went above to inform Everson of the situation. A few minutes later, Everson was heading for the forward hold when he spotted O'Neill also going to the hold. Everson called out "No admittance," and at the same time fired a shot which passed through O'Neill's left thigh and severed an artery. O'Neill claimed he was merely going to get a drink of water when he was shot. Everson, O'Neill recalled later, appeared intoxicated. Everson claimed that O'Neill was about to throw a keg of gunpowder into the furnace in order to blow up the ship; when ordered on deck, O'Neill refused to move and Everson shot him. O'Neill observed that Everson's story was hardly applicable to a man with a wife and four children.[9]

Lord Lyons urged a prompt investigation, the release of O'Neill from prison, and redress for the "grievous wrongs" inflicted upon him. At Seward's request, Welles inquired into the case and reported Everson's position. Seward passed the information on to Lyons, suggesting that Everson was guiltless, but that orders had nevertheless been given for O'Neill's release. The American government took its time in freeing O'Neill; only after continued prodding by Lyons was O'Neill released after an incarceration of seven months—and even then with an intimation that he really deserved to be treated as a pirate.[10]

The English government considered Everson's story "grossly improbable." The only one to assert that O'Neill intended to destroy the *Nicolai* and all aboard was Everson—the person guilty of inflicting the wound and with the strongest motive for exonerating himself from a charge of "savage brutality." The English, therefore, demanded a searching investigation by the Union government. Welles, pressed by Seward, reluctantly agreed to hold a trial.[11]

A Naval general court-martial, held at the navy yard in New York, charged Everson with assault with intent to kill as well as with maltreatment and cruelty. The testimony on whether or not Everson was intoxicated was conflicting; however, the Union officer who had spoken with O'Neill just before the shooting felt that there was nothing in O'Neill's manner or conduct that could have reasonably caused Everson any apprehension. The court found Everson guilty and sentenced him to imprisonment for a year, deprivation of his pay during that period and, at the end of his imprisonment, dismissal from the Navy. Justice was most likely served, and the British probably could not have asked for a more satisfactory conclusion. The American government failed to grant compensation to O'Neill, but this was the usual story when neutrals seized aboard blockade-runners were released.[12]

The seizure of the *Victor* in May 1863 brought loud cries of protest from the captured British subjects. The master, mate, and engineer of the *Victor* made numerous claims: they had been treated as prisoners of war or as felons; they were held aboard an American warship for over a week and compelled to sleep on a bare deck; they had been placed in a dungeon without circulating air and in which there was intense heat and a myriad of mosquitoes; and they were denied adequate time to eat and were refused communication with a British Vice-Consul. American naval officers, on the other hand, claimed that the men had been detained aboard the American ship until they could be examined by a court, that they had been well cared for, given beds and complete freedom of the ship. When the warship was ready for sea, the neutrals were lodged in a fort for a few days where there was freely circulating air, where the men had as much time as they desired to eat, and where they had opportunity to communicate with the British Vice-Consul; they had been treated neither as prisoners of war nor as felons. The law officers of the Crown and the Foreign Office accepted the American position and dropped the case, as they did in similar situations.[13]

The English were hardly satisfied, however. In an interview with President Lincoln to discuss American violations of neutral territory, Lyons observed that although the instructions issued by the Navy Department were acceptable, in practice captured neutrals were often treated as criminals. Lincoln admitted the truth of the allegations and noted also that there had been a lack of understanding of the diplomatic importance of prize cases—that these cases affected the relations between governments and even encompassed questions of war and peace. Lyons suggested that, under the American governmental system, the President could step in and direct affairs. As a result, Lincoln suggested to Welles on July 25, 1863, that he instruct naval commanders not to detain captured neutrals, except for the small number necessary as witnesses in the prize courts. This would re-emphasize the government's position. Welles replied that it was best to send in all prisoners because one could not tell who was a neutral and who was a rebel and that there was neither authority nor precedent for the instructions submitted by Lincoln. No further instructions were issued at that time.[14]

As the war was intensified and the number of blockade-runners increased, the Union treatment of captured neutrals became more rigorous. The officers and crew of the *Banshee*, which was taken while attempting to enter Wilmington, were detained over two months. All but one member of the captured crew had run the blockade before, so they knew what to do. They pressed the British government to obtain their release, complaining that they could not understand the reason for their detention, that the captain was seriously sick and that all of the crew were sick more or less, that they were required to pay their own board and medical bills, and that a local judge offered to have them released if they paid him $100. It seemed strange to one prisoner that money could absolve someone from an alleged crime in America, while one's guilt or innocence was not considered.[15]

In answer to Lyons' complaint, Seward charged that released blockade-runners had utilized their freedom to perform murders and acts of piracy within the harbors and on board ships of the United States. It had therefore been deemed necessary to institute a rigorous investigation into the character of all persons found on board ships captured while violating the blockade before they could be set at liberty. Such an investigation had been made in the case of the officers and crew of the *Banshee*. In addition to being suspected of attempting to run the blockade, it was also believed that the vessel might have been a Confederate cruiser. The inquiry revealed that the vessel was English and was only engaged in running the blockade. Thirty-nine of the forty persons involved would be released as neutral subjects; the exception was an insurgent. All of the men released would be held under "vigilant surveillance as dangerous persons." They would be expected to leave the United States within fifteen days after their discharge from custody. The character of blockade-runners captured thereafter would be subject to similar treatment. The British denied the validity of Seward's reasons, but nevertheless the case was closed.[16]

By 1864 the British were becoming seriously annoyed—and they had steadily increasing justification. Lyons suspected that Seward and his colleagues were trying to produce as much consternation among the blockade-runners as possible before getting into serious difficulty with foreign powers. Lyons pressed Seward to improve the treatment of blockade-runners, but he felt Seward lacked influence with Welles and Stanton. Perhaps partly to conceal his lack of power, Seward seemed to be making light of Lyons' grievances—or so Lyons thought. In mid-1864 Lyons moaned to Russell, "I am out of heart altogether." But Russell was determined that if the American government wished to remain on good terms with the government of England, their representatives had best keep their hands off English subjects.[17]

The Americans, of course, had reasons for treating blockade-runners strictly. Seward mentioned some of them in the correspondence regarding the *Banshee* prisoners, but there were others. The obvious fact that the runners were aiding the Confederates by supplying sustenance for their struggle was a contributing factor to the kind of treatment they received. Some of the runners were spies in the employment of the Southern government; when released by a prize court after giving testimony, they sometimes gathered intelligence in the United States for the Confederate government.[18]

On January 11, 1864, following the discovery of incriminating letters aboard the captured blockade-runners *Cornubia* and *Robert E. Lee* from English shipbuilders and merchants to the Confederate government, Seward suggested to Welles that such incidents provided ample reason to keep English blockade-runners in custody. Welles issued the following order on the same day: "Henceforth British blockade violators will not be released, but detained, and any orders which you may have received inconsistent with this are hereby revoked." Lyons learned of the order through an article in the New York *Herald;* he wrote Seward that he had received the information with "pain and alarm," and expressed his hope that Seward would either deny the validity or explain the meaning of the report.[19] Seward, hardly taken aback, replied that the report was entirely unofficial and unauthorized.

According to Seward, British subjects had been engaged in military expeditions against the United States from Canada; that parties in Richmond, Liverpool, New York, and Halifax had matured a plan in late December to seize two steamers sailing from New York on the high seas, arm them in Britain, and use them against the United States; that conspirators were even now organizing naval warfare against the United States under the shield of British neutrality; that the Confederates possessed several military transports, built or bought in English ports and navigated by English subjects, which were carrying supplies to the rebel forces under the English flag on the false pretense of being neutral traders engaged in simple violations of blockade.

Seward further stated that many persons engaged in these hostile activities had been captured one or more times as blockade-runners and, after a hasty examination, had been discharged on the false plea that they were lawful and peaceful subjects of a neutral, friendly power. The continuation of the aggressions described "must bring on border collisions and war between her Majesty's colonies and the United States." The American government had taken a number of steps to prevent aggressions; part of this effort included the detention of all persons entering the insurgent lines with munitions and supplies until a thorough investigation of their cases had been made, in order to ascertain whether they were neutral aliens or belligerent enemies. Truly neutral blockade-runners would be released as soon as possible, while the belligerent enemies found among the runners would be detained. The investigation would be conducted in such a manner as to subject lawful and peaceful persons to as little inconvenience as possible.[20]

While Seward and Welles kept British nerves on edge in Washington, Charles Francis Adams tried to do the same in London. Hoping to persuade the English government to keep its people from blockade-running, Adams wrote Russell at the end of January that all British subjects engaged in blockade-running incurred a suspicion strong enough to make them liable for treatment as enemies, and if seized, for consideration as prisoners of war. Unless the English government interfered with such activities as Confederate purchases of English vessels, manning those vessels with British seamen, filling them with supplies obtained in British ports, and violating the blockade under protection of the Union Jack, the "duty of self-defence, against such a policy of disguised hostility, becomes imperative." It was no longer clear, Adams noted, which vessels were owned by Englishmen and which by Confederates; all must be suspect and their crews treated as enemies on capture. Captured blockade-runners must now be presumed guilty until they could prove otherwise. To strengthen his case, Adams cited a Confederate law which required that half the tonnage of each vessel engaged in trade with Southern ports could be utilized by the Confederate government. Hence, all vessels engaged in the trade took on enemy character. British subjects entering that trade had to be considered as having changed their neutral character and as having become "allies and servants to the Insurgents" in carrying on the war. Lord Russell objected in vain to Adams' arguments.[21]

By May 1864 it had become apparent to Lyons that the system adopted by the United States permitted it to inflict long imprisonment on neutral subjects as a penalty for involvement in blockade-running; the justification given for this policy was the investigation of the validity of the captured men's claims to foreign protection.[22] Lyons persisted in his efforts to have imprisoned crews released and to change the treatment of neutrals by the Union government. He seemed to have made some progress.

On May 9 the Navy Department issued comprehensive instructions which were intended to satisfy the demands of the English government. Foreigners captured in neutral ships were to be released immediately, except those needed as witnesses, and the latter would be freed as soon as their testimony was taken; foreigners taken while serving aboard a vessel which lacked papers or a flag would be detained until the ship's neutrality was satisfactorily established; and those whose citizenship was in question would be required, before their release, to swear that they were not citizens of the United States and that they had never been in the employment of the Confederate government.[23]

Her Majesty's law officers received the instructions with great satisfaction, observing that the new rules indicated a return of the United States government to the true principles of international law and that the instructions seemed to place the questions in their proper perspective, at least on paper.[24]

American practice, however, continued to contradict

paper principles. On May 16 Seward forwarded to Lyons a note penned by Welles four days after the directions had been issued. Welles commented that bona fide British subjects taken aboard blockade-runners were to be released after they had served as witnesses and if they were not charged with belligerent acts. But, Welles continued, doubtful cases frequently arose; further examination or the production of additional evidence was at times necessary. It was not unreasonable to expect that blockade-violators would be subjected to detentions and annoyances; the cause in which they were engaged was certainly not one which commended them to special favor or hasty action. Welles was not alone in his views.[25]

Seward wrote Lyons on May 31 that blockade-runners were employing every artifice and fraud which promised to conceal their nationality, the unlawful character of their voyage, and the nationality of their vessels. They simulated flags, erased names, threw papers overboard or burned them, prevaricated and equivocated and—be they neutral or rebel—generally claimed the rights of British subjects. If occasionally British subjects engaging in an unlawful trade were detained for a thorough investigation, their misfortune resulted from their own fraudulent or suspicious conduct which violated both international law and the laws of their own nations. Their detention would last only so long as was necessary for careful and diligent examination.[26] The statements of Welles and Seward and the continuation of lengthy detentions of neutrals made clear that the British should not rely on the directions of May 9.

Anglo-American relations again became tense after an incident which occurred aboard the British bark *Saxon*. The vessel was seized on the west coast of Africa by the U.S.S. *Vanderbilt* for possession of American property which had been seized from a United States merchantman by a Confederate cruiser. The *Saxon's* crew became uneasy after the captain was arrested for resisting the prize master's orders regarding the disposal of meat on board the ship. James Gray, second mate on the *Saxon*, was ascending a ladder from the main deck to the poop when Acting Master's Mate Charles Danenhower of the *Vanderbilt* ordered him down and threatened to shoot him if he did not obey; Danenhower then pushed Gray, causing him to lose his balance. Gray fell back but swung around while attempting to recover his balance, and Danenhower fired a single mortal shot. This English version of the incident was described by the English press as an "almost unparalleled act of ruffianism" and as "the climax of outrage and atrocity." [27]

In response to Lyons' demand for an immediate investigation and the rendering of "prompt and effectual justice," Welles ordered a naval court of inquiry. The receipt of further evidence caused the British government to demand that Danenhower be tried for murder. The court of inquiry, however, exonerated Danenhower from the charge of unjustifiable homicide. Welles opposed a court martial which, he said, could only reflect injuriously upon the officers who had rendered the acquittal verdict; furthermore, it would unnecessarily subject Danenhower to fresh suspicion, expense, and inconvenience. There was no reason to suppose that a court martial finding would in any way differ from that of the court of inquiry. The British did not relent, Seward pressed Welles, and the *New York Times* urged that a formal trial would be best for the national reputation—that men who were exercising power over life and death ought to realize that the law stood above them.[28] Welles gave in.

The General Court Martial which convened at the Philadelphia Naval Yard indicted Danenhower for murdering James Gray "willfully, feloniously," and with "malice aforethought." The court also charged Danenhower with manslaughter. The defendant argued that the shooting was unintentional and accidental, that Gray had been trying to push him out of the way and he had been trying to prevent Gray's progress up the ladder when the pistol discharged. The defendant further argued that Gray had resisted his authority, which was an act of mutiny, and had thereby subjected himself to any measure required to suppress that act; in fact, under a law passed in July of 1862, it was Danenhower's duty to use his utmost effort to suppress insubordination and mutiny. Even if the killing had been intentional, it would still have been legally justified. Certainly there had been no malice whatsoever felt toward Gray. Danenhower had attempted to prevent Gray's ascent because it seemed he was going to obtain arms which were stored in a cabin on the poop deck in order to carry out an act of mutiny. Danenhower also considered himself directly threatened and was only resorting to the right of self-defense in opposing Gray's effort.[29]

The court, after hearing the evidence, found Danenhower innocent of both murder and manslaughter. Seward passed the verdict to Lyons, adding that as a consequence of the decision, there was no responsibility on the part of the United States government. The British government was "on the whole" of the opinion that the finding of the court had to be accepted as conclusive, although it was thought that the American government might voluntarily make some compensation to the relations of Gray, whose life had been "so needlessly sacrificed by the impetuosity and carelessness of one of their officers." [30]

The widow of James Gray pressed the Foreign Office to obtain compensation for her, arguing that her husband had been deprived of his life without provocation by the American officer and that she was entirely destitute, with four children to provide for. The British chargé d'affaires, J. Hume Burnley, suggested to Seward that the American government should provide some compensation for the widow.[31]

Seward reminded Burnley rather brusquely of the result of the court martial and told him that Gray had been voluntarily engaged for his own gain in an enterprise which was hostile and injurious to the United States, in violation of international law and in disobedience to the express command of his sovereign. Charity in such a case would tend to increase rather than diminish the already too great number of those foreigners who, like Gray, were seduced by cupidity into hostile actions and illicit enterprises against the United States. As a consequence, no compensation was forthcoming.[32]

The case of the *Night Hawk* further piqued British sensibilities. The *Night Hawk* ran aground off Wilmington while attempting to run the blockade of that port. A boat's crew from the U.S.S. *Niphon* approached the vessel, firing several volleys of small arms fire and wounding the *Night Hawk's* surgeon, a seaman, and a fireman. Within three minutes of boarding the vessel and without examining the ship's papers, the Americans set fire to her. When the *Night Hawk's* chief engineer asked the boarding officer for permission to retrieve some of his possessions, the officer struck him in the face with a pistol, inflicting a serious wound. Several of the *Night Hawk's* officers and crew had escaped when the boarding party approached, twenty-three others were taken off by the Americans, and fourteen were left aboard the burning ship to fare for themselves—an unhappy situation to be in, considering that the vessel carried a quantity of gunpowder. So went the English story. Burnley protested the treatment of noncombatant and unresisting neutrals as prisoners of war, the wounding of the men, the burning of the ship, and the detention of the crew; he demanded an immediate inquiry.[33]

Seward responded to the British complaints with a note from Welles which presented the American side. According to Welles, shots had been fired by the boarding party, but only at a group escaping from the *Night Hawk* as the boarders approached the ship. Shortly after the Americans boarded the vessel, the rebel batteries at Fort Fisher opened fire upon the *Night Hawk* and the *Niphon*. Because of their exposure to this gunfire and because of their inability to free the blockade-runner, the Americans set her afire, taking with them to the *Niphon* those of the officers and crew who had not escaped to shore. The ship was in all likelihood rebel-owned or at least running on behalf of the Confederate government, and her officers and crew were probably rebels. The only men from the *Hawk* who might have been wounded were those who were escaping when the *Niphon's* boat approached; at the time it had been impossible for the Americans to know whether those escaping were neutrals or enemies.[34]

The British government remained unmoved. Under British pressure, Welles ordered a naval court of inquiry. The court supported the American position, although without confirming that the *Night Hawk* or its officers and crew were rebels. The engineer had been struck because, at the time he made his request, there were only eight Americans surrounded by twenty-five to thirty men from the *Night Hawk*; hesitation might have jeopardized American lives and possession of the vessel. While some of the *Hawk's* men were left on board the burning ship, they were able to and did reach shore in one of her boats. The court concluded that the destruction of the *Night Hawk* was "justifiable and necessary" and that there was no misconduct on the part of the boarding party.[35]

The English were not at all pleased with the trial or with the detention of the *Night Hawk's* men, the last of whom were not finally released until three months after their seizure. The inquiry was a farce, the British contended, for the only persons called as witnesses were those whose conduct was under investigation; the officers of the *Hawk* were kept in prison and their evidence was not even asked for, being in effect suppressed. The English hoped to see justice done in the case. Seward replied cryptically that the case would receive "proper consideration," and that was the end of it.[36]

The Union gained strength as the war progressed; it became obvious that England would not intervene forcefully in the treatment of neutrals or in any other matter, so the American government pressed its advantage. The blockade by 1865 had become almost impenetrable and hundreds of sailors once involved in blockade-running were unemployed. Some found themselves in the United States. The *New York Times* considered them "insolent in proportion to their filth and raggedness, and they fancy that their flag is specially intended to cover insolence." [37]

In mid-March President Lincoln ordered foreigners who had been or were engaged in blockade-running to leave the country within twelve days of his order or twelve days after their arrival in the United States. They were not to return during the continuance of the war and would be imprisoned if they violated the order. The British again protested that neutral persons involved in blockade-running could only be detained temporarily as witnesses. Seward replied that there was no law requiring a country engaged in a civil war to grant asylum to those who aided the enemy. Lincoln's order remained in effect; the war ended one month after its issuance.[38]

An examination of the treatment of neutrals by the Union government during the Civil War reveals that they fared none too well. In many cases, neutrals taken aboard blockade-runners were detained only as witnesses for short periods and then released. But there were numerous cases in which detentions were unduly lengthy, when the rules of international law were either stretched or violated, and when Union justice seemed a willing complement to the Union war effort. On the other hand, the Americans had good reason for treating seized neutrals with some harshness, even in violation of international law. Probably the most important reason was to deter blockade-runners from persisting in their trade. This goal was never realized, however, and the British did not consider the American justifications satisfactory. The questionable cases only served to exacerbate Anglo-American relations.

Why the English failed to act vigorously is not entirely clear. If they had openly threatened war over the mistreatment of English subjects, the Union would probably have desisted. Yet the British government spoke only moderately loud and without the benefit of any conspicuously big stick. When the State Department or the naval courts found the evidence of English subjects unworthy of consideration or false, the English government either accepted the decision or challenged it without force. Lengthy discourses on the nature of international law in no way menaced the Union war effort; Seward could engage in them indefinitely and Welles—the bête noire of Anglo-American relations during the Civil War —assisted him with arguments. For the English also, lengthy arguments were preferable, although they would not have admitted it. The English government had no desire to be dragged into a war with the United States by profit-minded subjects who placed their own needs over those of their nation. Her Majesty's government had more to be concerned with than a handful of adventurous subjects.

10

Great Britain
Looks at the Prize Cases

THERE have been many studies of English attitudes toward the American Civil War; these studies have been important, for they have attempted to reveal the reasons for England's failure to intervene. The numerous examinations have
probed the views of English leaders; of the upper, middle, and
lower classes; of certain interest groups and of peoples located
in various sections of Great Britain. They have also explored
the influence of wheat and cotton imports into Britain; the
role of English war profits; British attitudes toward democracy, aristocracy, slavery, liberty, and national self-determination; the opinions of the English press; and the role of Machiavellian calculation of national interests.[1] Curiously, there
has been no thorough analysis of the British attitudes toward
the Civil War prize cases, other than the *Trent* incident,
though English interests were very much involved in terms
of profits and losses, in terms of the possibility of war with

the United States, and in terms of the long-range needs of England as the principal maritime power.*

English newspapers reflected the views of all classes and every shade of political opinion relating to the Civil War prize cases. Of all the journals, the politically neutral *Shipping and Mercantile Gazette* of London dealt most extensively with the cases. Anything jeopardizing English trade elicited the most venomous articles, and American seizures and condemnations seemed to fit that category. The *Gazette* found that American judges were eager to condemn English ships "upon any possible legal quibble or technicality." Emotive terms flourished in the columns of the *Gazette:* trade between neutral ports was "sacred" and the shooting of the second mate of the British merchantman *Saxon* by an American naval officer was an act of "unredeemed atrocity." British commerce was continually threatened, it seemed, and was in fact being transferred to foreign vessels. Naval convoys were called on to protect legitimate trade. The *Gazette* was appalled by the government's apparent inaction: "The time has come for our Government and that of France to unite in such a representation to the Cabinet of Washington as will compel a respect for neutral rights. If this fail, we are surely strong enough to protect our lawful Commerce against molestation or interference." [2]

The Times of London, England's leading journal and a Whig organ, favored the Confederates but tended to be calculating and permissive toward the Union. The actions of the

* Over four decades ago James P. Baxter, III, pointed out that the response of the British government to the prize cases was largely dictated by the future interests of British sea power. This position is accurate as far as it goes, but Baxter's interest was limited to the Admiralty and Foreign office response to the cases; he too easily dismissed the extremely important sectors of public opinion, Parliamentary comment, and the role of domestic politics. See "The British Government and Neutral Rights, 1861–1865," *American Historical Review*, XXXIV (October, 1928), 9–29.

Union navy (notably Charles Wilkes) could bring *The Times* to try intimidation, as in the *Peterhoff* seizure, yet it recognized that expansion of belligerent maritime rights by the United States could only serve future British interests: "The Federals . . . are fighting our battles as well as their own." And *The Times* had little use for blockade-runners: "We shall not go to war . . . to avenge the injured innocence of men engaged in a mercantile lottery."[3]

The *Standard* of London, a Tory paper hostile to the Whig government and to the United States, produced columns which were consistently ultra-patriotic. The honor of the flag and the safety of English commerce had to be defended at all costs, according to the *Standard*. One issue decried the "Northern maritime Filibusters" who relied upon a "buccaneering license" to employ "a species of naval terrorism" against British shipping. Although the foreign secretary, Lord Russell, had "submitted tamely to and even tacitly endorsed the grossest infringements of neutral rights," it was in fact his duty to make clear to the Federals that a continuation of their policy designed to stop legitimate trade would be treated as a *casus belli*. Yet the expression of such views in the *Standard* must come as no surprise; its editor opened the paper's columns, including the editorial section, to Henry Hotze, the chief Confederate propagandist in Europe and the editor of the *Index*, the rebel propaganda organ published in London.[4]

Other London newspapers exhibited a variety of viewpoints. One of the chief Whig dailies, the *Morning Post*, which was a mouthpiece for Prime Minister Palmerston, thought that American naval officers had behaved with "great rigour" toward neutral commerce because of American jealousy of British commercial and naval ascendancy and because of "desperate necessity." Even if belligerent rights were stretched to their fullest extent, the *Morning Post*, like *The*

Times, felt this might eventually work to England's advantage. "We are not desirous of going to war," the *Morning Post* contended, "but it seems scarcely expedient to act as if we were afraid of being called upon to vindicate our independence by force of arms." Manly talk while looking to the future was the *Morning Post's* prescription.[5]

The Liberal *Globe and Traveller* of London, fearing that the Union would come to regard and treat bona fide neutrals as enemies, urged Englishmen to do nothing provocative and promoted a policy of forbearance and moderation consistent with neutral rights. The pro-Union *Daily News,* a liberal-radical journal, held that there was "not a more respectable, abler, or more learned or more independent body of men in the world" than the American prize court judges, and the *Daily News* depicted Englishmen who would prolong a conflict profitable to themselves as "Mammon-worshippers." Yet even the *Daily News* warned that Washington leaders were "grievously mistaken if they suppose that there is any party in this country who will counsel submission to any invasion of British rights." The radical *Spectator* and the independent *Army and Navy Gazette* called for an observance of international law both by England and by the United States. The *Economist,* a liberal-independent journal written primarily for members of commercial and financial circles, was hostile to the North and considered the appointment of Wilkes to the command of the West India Squadron "to surpass the recognized limits of human incapacity." [6]

The papers of Liverpool, one of the principal English shipping ports, not surprisingly tended to feel strongly about any interferences with British trade by Union cruisers. The *Liverpool Courier,* a Tory newspaper, was certainly one of the most jingoistic of the English papers, saying everything possible which would bring England and the United States to war. Editorials had such titles as "WAR OR PEACE" and "THE

NORTH WANTS CANADA." The *Liverpool Courier* insisted that Englishmen must cease singing "Rule Britannia" while Lord Russell remained in the Foreign Office and that the hands of British naval officers were tied with the "red-tapery of an imbecile and cowardly Administration."

It was much easier and more lucrative for Union naval vessels "to pounce upon an unarmed merchant ship" than to deal with Confederate cruisers or to attack the Confederate coasts, continued the *Courier*. The Union government in all likelihood wanted war with England: such a conflict might unite the hostile parties in America, allow a pretext under cover of which the South might be set free, and gain Vancouver and British Columbia, if not all of Canada, for the United States. If the "piracy" committed upon English commerce in the West Indies went unpunished, there would soon be a cordon of Federal cruisers lying in wait for English vessels outside the Mersey. "With people who act by the law of force," concluded the *Liverpool Courier*, "the law of force is the only remedy." [7]

Other Liverpool newspapers, while not as chauvinistic as the *Courier*, also spoke out vigorously. The *Liverpool Mercury*, one of the most influential Liberal newspapers in the north of England, regarded Wilkes as "an ill-informed and violent-tempered naval officer" who could be relied upon "to vex, harass, and insult English traders carrying on a lawful neutral traffic." The blockade of the South must not be allowed to include Matamoros. While there was often justification for the seizure and condemnation of English merchantmen, the American government must at all times abide by international law. The *Liverpool Mercury* concluded that "a prudent and resolute bearing will obtain the pacific redress of international wrongs for which law and justice—not to speak of courtesy and friendship—might plead in vain." [8]

Gore's General Advertiser, a nonpolitical commercial

and shipping paper, maintained that the English government should not pledge itself to protect English vessels involved in an illicit trade, but that the "despicable practice of maritime garrotting" could not be long tolerated. *Gore's General Advertiser* was confident that "a bold policy is the conservator of peace, a timid one, the provocative of war." [9]

Journals in other shipping and manufacturing centers also exhibited a variety of viewpoints. The Liberal *Manchester Guardian* favored "a judicious mixture of firmness and courtesy" and a recognition of the problems faced by the United States. Many of the complaints made by English shippers were "ignorant and unreasonable," and the *Manchester Guardian* knew of no incident which could not be amicably settled between England and America. The Liberal *Southampton Times* also desired the dispassionate settlement of differences, for "the interests of both nations—the welfare of the human race—are wrapped up in the word—PEACE. Long may it be preserved." The independent *Falmouth and Penryn Weekly Times and General Advertiser* concurred in this view and hoped that warmongers would hold their tongues. The *Sheffield and Rotherham Independent*, a Liberal journal, contended that Lord Russell was acting in England's best interests by not straining neutral rights, for it was not to England's advantage to cripple belligerent rights. [10]

Although England might expect that there would be no seizures of English vessels without sufficient cause, the radical *Newcastle Daily Chronicle* did not choose to rush into a war with the United States because certain English capitalists found blockade-running to be profitable. *Aris's Birmingham Gazette*, an independent weekly, insisted that while England should in all respects maintain its neutrality during the American Civil War, she should "act promptly, vigorously, even fiercely, whenever another nation dares to attempt even the slightest infringements of our rights." The radical *Birming-*

ham Journal recognized that "great skill and forbearance, mingled with not a little firmness," would be required to conduct Anglo-American relations in such a manner as to maintain peace.[11]

Discussions and debates in Parliament revealed much irritation with the actions of American cruisers and courts and with the apparent inaction of the Palmerston ministry. Ulick John De-Burgh, Marquess of Clanricarde, was a pro-Confederate Tory and a close friend of the Southern commissioner in London. He proclaimed in the House of Lords that the Union government and its officers had been acting under a design to stop the legitimate trade of England; war must follow unless Her Majesty's government acted in "a firm but temperate manner." Lord Robert Cecil, a powerful Conservative and a leading promoter of Southern independence, announced in the House of Commons that the American courts had delivered their judgments "under the pressure of fixed bayonets." Cecil attacked the Liberal government's policy and, in response to the shooting aboard the *Saxon*, demanded "to see some of the energy displayed at Kagosima" by the Royal Navy used against the United States. Seymour Fitzgerald, another Conservative advocate of Southern independence, criticized in the House of Commons the "total disregard of other powers" by naval officers of the United States while Cavendish Bentinck, likewise a pro-South Tory, attacked the English government directly. Lord Palmerston had no qualms about the employment of force against "a feeble adversary," Bentinck pointed out, but "when he had to meet 'the great Abraham,' he bent low, and in a bondman's key, with bated breath and whispering humbleness, said, 'Fair Sir, you spit on me on Wednesday last; you spurned me such a day, and for these courtesies I now obey your bidding.'" British honor required vindication.[12]

Most, but not all, criticisms in Parliament were made by

members of the pro-Confederate wing of the Tory party. They hoped to pressure the Palmerston government into harassing and hurting, perhaps provoking, the Union government and thereby to aid the South. Although responsible Conservatives preferred a policy of neutrality for England in its relation to the American Civil War, some members of their party attacked the Palmerston government for political reasons. Since the Conservative party was in the minority in the first half of the 1860's, Tories at times attempted to embarrass and discredit the Liberal government and to ingratiate themselves with the British public. These Conservatives hoped that their efforts would bear fruit in the next election. Under these circumstances, it is necessary to examine the real significance of the criticism leveled at the Americans and at the Palmerston ministry in its approach to the Union government.[13]

While the motives of the Parliamentary critics may not have been entirely pure, the critics were taken seriously, as if their first concern was indeed the rights of Englishmen. Members of the British press watched closely the discussions in Parliament, and they often published their own views on the remarks made. There were few defenders in Parliament of the Palmerston ministry's response to the prize cases. Leading representatives of the administration, such as the Prime Minister and Lord Russell, had to personally answer the critics. Other Liberals remained silent.

The opinions of the English press, the comments of the Conservative members of Parliament, and the silence of the Liberals made plain that if Englishmen did not feel overtly hostile to the United States for its real and alleged violations of neutral rights, they were seriously irritated by them. The highest degree of discussion and antagonistic feeling toward the Union resulting from the prize cases appeared at the end of April and early May 1863 during the *Peterhoff* crisis. It was then that hostile attitudes rose to the surface over a number of alleged violations of English rights and insults to British honor which had been taking place over a long period of time but which were suddenly occurring in the most flagrant manner and in concentration: the seizure of neutral ships traveling between neutral ports on the basis of the "untenable" doctrine of continuous voyage; the following to sea and capturing of English merchantmen by Union warships based in neutral ports; the various activities of Charles Wilkes; and the issuance by the American minister in London of a letter of reference for American traders. English honor, commerce, and the very role of Great Britain as mistress of the seas appeared to be at stake. A war crisis was at hand, and it was not a secret to anyone.

The American Consul General in Paris, John Bigelow, visited London during the second half of April 1863 to relieve his anxiety about an Anglo-American war. He reported to Seward: "With a good chance of a short and successful war with the United States, I doubt if the British Ministry could find more popular employment." The Confederate commissioner in London, James M. Mason, wrote the Southern Secretary of State that a strong opinion was prevailing that it would be difficult to avoid drifting into the war which the Lincoln government seemed determined to provoke. Others presented their own interpretations of the crisis, but the most comprehensive view of Northern thinking was that of the English minister in Washington, Lord Lyons.[14]

Lyons wrote Russell that there was indeed a serious danger of war with the United States. Americans were thoroughly exasperated with England because of the actions of English blockade-runners and the fitting out of Confederate cruisers in England. Union naval officers were a threat to peace, some desiring a war with England in order to get away from the dull work of blockading. Like most other Americans, the officers of the Navy Department were profoundly ignorant of the relative strength of England and America. It seemed to Lyons that William H. Seward, the American Secretary of State, had for a time fanned the flames in order to recover his lost popularity, but that now he wanted peace. Yet if strong measures became the Republican party cry, Seward could do little. If the North won no victories against the Southern forces, the more ardent Republicans would go to the verge of war with England to gain popularity. And there were some who said that if the South was going to be lost, the best way to conceal Republican guilt would be to go to war with England and attribute the loss of the South to English interference. So far as the danger of war with England was concerned, Lyons believed that the situation in America was more alarming than it had been at any time since the *Trent* affair.[15]

Reports on all sides suggested that a war with the United States was in the offing; it was not until May 22 that English opinion was reported to be "recovering its senses." [16] Responsible members of the American government were certainly not considering a war with Great Britain at this time, and they would hardly have been wise to do so. The question must then arise about the attitudes of Her Majesty's government, for the declaration of such a war would have to come from them. This question can best be explored in terms of their attitudes throughout the Civil War rather than just during the crisis of April–May 1863. The English government recognized dangers throughout the Civil War.

The most fundamental feeling of the key members of the British government was the desire to remain neutral and to take advantage of Northern belligerent pretensions. Her Majesty proclaimed on May 13, 1861: "We do hereby strictly charge and command all our loving subjects to observe a strict neutrality." Lord Palmerston, the Prime Minister, wrote Russell in October 1861 that England's best course was to con-

tinue as she had begun, "to keep quite clear of the conflict."
He felt that the British should give the Americans no reason
for quarrel and at the same time they should maintain English
rights. Attacked in Parliament for following a policy of "bullying the weak and truckling to the strong," Palmerston in February of 1864 denied the assertion and pointed out that there
was no reason to doubt the fairness and independence of
American courts; he further noted that the Union government had "invariably received our representations in a spirit
of respect, equity, and justice." [17]

English precedents and anticipated needs of English sea
power dictated a conciliatory policy toward the North. As
the law officers of the Crown stated at the end of June 1862,
in reference to English vessels captured or condemned, "the
presumption should always be in favour of the legality and
justice of the belligerent proceedings." Yet the Palmerston
government hardly followed a policy of "truckling" to the
United States, for as the law officers advised, the English government did intervene on behalf of its subjects in cases of
"manifest wrong and injury, shewing an abuse of the belligerent powers and rights." [18]

Looking back upon the Civil War a decade after it had
ended, Lord Russell confessed that the British government
was "far from pressing hard on the United States and, in spite
of remonstrances from many quarters, put no impediment in
the way of the capture of British merchant ships." During the
war, however, alleged violations of neutral rights by the
Union government could bring Russell to say that he would
"be ready to meet the Yankees if they take to bullying." [19]
Yet Russell's attitude, like Palmerston's, was essentially conciliatory.

Although he could write privately that American cap-
tains were insolent and that "I suspect the U. S. Justice is
bad," in Parliament Russell contended that the activities of

English blockade-runners had certainly given the Americans ample justification for making seizures, that Seward fully acknowledged the principles of international law, and that the law officers had found no grounds for complaint in American prize judgments. In a letter to the English owners of a vessel seized by the Union navy, Russell said that Her Majesty's government could not "deny in this war the exercise of those rights which, in all wars in which Great Britain had been concerned, she had claimed herself to exercise." He advised Liverpool merchants and shipowners who complained about American interference with their trade in the Bahamas to "refrain from this species of trade." When Russell thought the war fever was on the rise in England and America, he expressed the following hope to Lyons: "May both nations cool down from this insane fury before it is too late!" Russell did what he could in England and directed Lyons and the British chargé d'affaires in Washington to work with Seward and Lincoln for Anglo-American peace.[20]

Lyons was the principal English link between the two governments when the prize cases came under discussion. Russell relied upon what he considered to be Lyons' "wisdom, patience, and prudence" to keep England out of war. Lyons strongly sympathized with the North at the commencement of the war; yet he was increasingly vexed by American behavior. Lyons complained to Russell in July of 1864 that cases of imprisonment of British subjects, interference with trade, and "wrongs of all kinds" had become "the labour of my life." The British minister's interference in prize cases seemed to bring him nothing "but snubs." Something had to be done however: there was "so much wrong-headedness at the Navy Department" that its proceedings were a danger to peaceful relations. Lyons certainly did his part to maintain good relations with the United States and at the same time worked hard to maintain the rights of Englishmen.[21]

Although Lyons followed closely Russell's instructions and pressed hard upon Seward's arguments, his requests and his wording could not be construed to mean that the United States had the option of meeting English demands or going to war. He earnestly wanted peace with the United States; he advised one of his temporary replacements in the Washington legation to avoid "all risk of getting up an excitement on doubtful or small cases. After the mischief is done public opinion always tones down and condemns those who made small causes produce great evils." Lyons understood well the limits beyond which he could not go; he acted with consummate skill in explosive times.[22]

The Admiralty reflected the views of the Foreign Office and followed Lord Russell's recommendations. The instructions issued to the commander of Her Majesty's warships on the North American and West India Station in February 1864 typified the moderate attitude of the Admiralty. The commander was ordered to be "extremely careful to maintain on all occasions a perfect neutrality," to be certain that his subordinates should in no way give "countenance to vessels under the British Flag which may be employed in any manner inconsistent with the Neutrality which Her Majesty has enjoined all Her Subjects to maintain during the Contest," to protect legitimate English trade, and to exercise forbearance in difficult times, referring serious problems to the home government for settlement.[23]

Vice-Admiral Sir Alexander Milne, in command of the British squadron on the North American and West India Station for most of the war and the one man who could most easily have permitted a war to break out, exhibited tact, impartiality, sound judgment, and legal knowledge. Milne's qualities were recognized by all who dealt with him, including President Lincoln, Secretary of the Navy Welles, and Secretary of State Seward. Lyons wrote in October of 1863 that the Union government recognized that "to nothing more than to the excellent judgment and to the firm but temperate and conciliatory conduct of the Admiral is owing the maintenance of harmonious relations between the two Countries." [24]

Milne kept a tight rein on his subordinates, many of whom displayed pro-Confederate sympathies, and he was often able to influence and shape policy according to his own interpretation of circumstances. For example, he squelched the demands of English shippers for naval convoys because he felt that convoys would only increase the likelihood of Anglo-American collisions. He ordered his officers to abstain from any act likely to involve England in hostilities with the United States. Although irritated by the ways in which belligerent rights were being exercised by the Americans, Milne wrote: "If we change positions with Adm. Wilkes, I dare say we would feel annoyed to see several steamers full of contraband of war in a harbour of a neutral port ready to break *our* blockade." [25]

With most English newspapers insisting on the firm maintenance of neutral rights and some journals advocating the resort to arms, with members of Parliament attacking the government for its allegedly spineless stand against the Americans, with talk of war in the air, a squall across the Atlantic persisted in varying degrees throughout the Civil War. For reasons of precedent and future requirements, and out of a desire to steer clear of the American conflict, the English government resisted the extreme demands of public opinion and refused to be swept away by the tempest. Yet it would be unfair to describe the actions taken by the Palmerston ministry as "appeasement." The Palmerston government argued continually, consistently, and extensively for the minimum respect due a neutral; it placed ships of the Royal Navy in position to defend neutral rights if they were violated flagrantly; and it attempted to calm volatile feelings at home. Domestic pressure in England did not bring about a war primarily because of the efforts of key members of the English government—and American officials never quite pushed them too far.

11

Conclusion

CONSIDERING the great interest of historians in the Civil War, it is surprising that the Civil War prize cases have been virtually overlooked. Maritime incidents involving the actions of Union naval officers, the maneuvers of Northern diplomats, and the rulings of American judges seriously aggravated Anglo-American relations at a time when the United States could ill afford another war. A conflict with England would probably have meant the secession of the Confederacy from the Union; it was the primary aim of the Lincoln government to prevent such an occurrence, which would have transformed the course of American history.

The seizures of vessels for intent to violate the blockade of the South and for carriage of contraband to the Confederacy were designed to prevent the Southern government from gaining or sustaining the power necessary to achieve its goal of secession. Union officials should have acted with skill, precision, and sensitivity in regard to neutrals, but such was not always the case. The Northern desire for victory over the

South often conflicted with the insistent demand of English traders for profits. Anglo-American relations suffered in consequence.

The English government recognized the validity of the Union blockade, but the owners of several vessels seized at the beginning of the war attacked its legality in the *Prize Cases*, at the same time raising questions with far-reaching implications for the Union war effort. If the Northern courts ruled against the validity of the blockade, Southern trade would be open and the rebellion might succeed. Fortunately for the Union, the Supreme Court ruled that the blockade and the capture of prizes were legal and that they could continue without legal impediment. At the same time, the *Prize Cases* sustained Lincoln's claim to extensive emergency powers which he felt he needed in order to win the war. The same cases encouraged the administration to add an additional justice, so that the Court could be more readily relied upon to serve the government.

The location of Matamoros, Mexico, across the Rio Grande from Brownsville, Texas, made it an ideal Confederate trade center. No legal blockade could be made of the Rio Grande, and trade between neutral European ports and neutral Matamoros could not be interrupted, according to existing interpretations of international law. The Union government did not accept this situation, and American naval officers seized vessels passing to and from Matamoros. As a result, Anglo-American disputes arose over the carriage of contraband between neutral ports as a basis for seizures, the location of captures, seizures irrespective of blockade or contraband, delays in Union prize courts, and costs and damages.

The *Labuan* case brought out a number of the problems which arose in the Matamoros cases and also revealed a reluctance on the part of the Union prize court to spell out any legal principles on which neutral traders could rely. Seward replied to British demands with evasion and procrastination, though he considered the seizure of the *Labuan* illegal. Evasion and delay could only fluster and confuse English traders, perhaps keeping them away from the Matamoros market. Delays resulting from further Federal investigations, Congressional opposition, and the unwillingness of the American government to pay some of the claims meant that all of the claims in the case were not finally settled until eleven and a half years after the seizure of the *Labuan*.

Other Matamoros captures increased Anglo-American tensions. In these cases, Union naval officers made captures of questionable legality. The Secretary of State professed American loyalty to the same principles of law to which England adhered and put off British protests by accusing England of aiding the South. In none of the Matamoros cases were the ships finally condemned. This failure to condemn suggests that the ships had been seized without any legal basis. The district court decisions in several of the cases also had no relation to the requirements of international law, although all of the vessels except the *Volante* were released by that court. Only the district court ruling in the *Will o' the Wisp* case was made on the grounds that there could be no contraband trade between neutrals. The Supreme Court confirmed this interpretation in the other cases, although the Navy Department and its officers did not accept it—and the Supreme Court itself came to support the actions of the Union navy. Neutral traders were only temporarily intimidated and the Matamoros-Brownsville trade continued to thrive, but not because of inaction on the part of the Union government and its officials.

If the Matamoros trade could not be prevented, because of legal hindrances, then perhaps the courts should remove those hindrances and alter the law to fit the needs of the Northern government. Such was the thought of Union naval officers and such became the thought of Union judges who condemned vessels and cargoes on the basis of the doctrine of continuous voyage, long in a state of disuse but now eminently usable.

The British public was furious at the employment of the doctrine, but the English government accepted America's interpretation of the concept because it could be useful to the mistress of the seas in future wars. But the English government and the public were angered by the *Peterhoff* mail incident and by the Adams certificate incident, and in both cases the American State Department gave in to British demands. The Supreme Court judgment in the *Peterhoff* case extended the number of articles accepted as absolute contraband. It was also probably the first ruling in which condemnation of a cargo was based upon application of the doctrine of continuous voyage to conditional contraband with an immediate neutral destination. The verdict was also the first significant ruling to condemn contraband intended for conveyance to a neutral port and then inland to a belligerent destination. All of the principal steps taken by the American government in the *Peterhoff* case, while not always in apparent alignment with each other, were unified by a desire for victory over the South, for peace with England, and for a position supported by international law.

In the *Springbok* case, the Supreme Court ruled that a cargo shipped with the intention of ultimate importation into a blockaded port could be seized at any point in its voyage, even if the cargo was to be transshipped at an intermediate neutral port. The penalty for breach of blockade was applied to a guilty cargo in an innocent ship; the *Springbok* was the first case in which a vessel was released while its cargo was condemned for breach of blockade. This case and other continuous voyage rulings went far toward making a blockade of enemy ports unnecessary by substituting what was in effect a paper blockade of neutral ports. England and other nations subsequent to the American Civil War occasionally based their own naval actions on America's employment of the doctrine of continuous voyage—and moved decidedly closer to the brutal reality of total war.

In addition to taking the "monstrous" step of utilizing the continuous voyage concept, Union officers violated the sovereignty of neutral states. They were accused of chasing, firing upon, burning, and seizing suspected blockade-runners in neutral territory, following suspected vessels from neutral ports in order to make captures, and blockading neutral ports. Naval zeal was incompatible with neutral rights, and neutral governments applied pressure on the State Department, just as the Navy Department put pressure on neutral traders.

The burning of the *Blanche* in Cuban waters raised the possibility of war with Spain. Charles Wilkes irritated the British and the Danes in a variety of ways, but most notably by his misuse of neutral ports as bases from which to follow neutral ships out to sea and to capture them. Union shells aimed at the *Margaret and Jessie* landed on British territory, aggravating Englishmen. Other such incidents complicated America's relations with foreign powers, especially England. Finally, under foreign pressure, a halt was called to violations of neutral territory.

The mistreatment of neutral subjects taken aboard blockade-runners by Union officials, like so many other developments arising from the prize cases, troubled Anglo-American relations. Such mistreatment was reinforced and given apparent justification by the rescue of the *Emily St. Pierre* and by the refusal of the English government to confiscate the vessel and return it to the Union government. Englishmen were placed in handcuffs and irons, closely confined, detained beyond the customary time needed to take testimony, treated as prisoners of war, required to make oaths, fired upon, wounded or killed, and expelled from American soil. These instances did not occur on a daily basis, but they did occur. Americans had many reasons for treating neutrals with severity, but Englishmen were unmoved and demanded decent treatment for neutral subjects.

Most English newspapers demanded the firm maintenance of neutral rights and some favored the use of force. Members of Parliament echoed these views. At the same time, there were voices of moderation, most notably among the key figures in the Palmerston administration who dealt with the cases. These men recognized that measures taken by the Union government at sea and in the courts had their foundation in English precedents and that those measures might be useful to England in a later conflict. In addition, there was an underlying desire to avoid active involvement in the American Civil War. The English government argued the cause of neutral rights firmly and interminably during the conflict, placed warships in a position to defend those rights if Union naval officers went far beyond the pale of law, and attempted to put a damper on combustible feelings at home. Yet the relationship between England and America, based upon the Civil War prize cases, cannot be regarded as peaceful; it was turbulent, producing a squall across the Atlantic.

NOTES

Notes

The following abbreviations are used in the Notes section.

PUBLISHED DOCUMENTS

OR — United States Department of the Army, *The War of the Rebellion: A Compilation of the Official Records of the Union and Confederate Armies* (128 vols., Washington, D.C., 1880–1901)

ORN — United States Navy Department, *Official Records of the Union and Confederate Navies in the War of the Rebellion* (29 vols., Washington, D.C., 1894–1922)

PRFA — United States Department of State, *Diplomatic Correspondence, Papers Relating to Foreign Affairs* (239 vols., Washington, D.C., 1861–1969)

DOCUMENTS IN THE PUBLIC RECORD OFFICE, LONDON

Adm.	Admiralty Papers
FO	Foreign Office Papers
PRO	Public Record Office Papers

DOCUMENTS IN THE NATIONAL MARITIME MUSEUM, GREENWICH

MLN	Milne Papers

DOCUMENTS IN THE NATIONAL ARCHIVES, WASHINGTON, D.C.

Despatches	Despatches from the United States minister in Great Britain to the Department of State
Diplomatic Instructions	Diplomatic Instructions of the State Department to the United States minister to Great Britain
Domestic Letters	Domestic Letters of the Department of State
Miscellaneous Letters	Miscellaneous Letters of the Department of State
Notes from the British Legation	Notes from the British Legation in the United States to the Department of State
Notes from the Department of State	Notes from the Department of State to foreign [British] ministers and consuls in the United States, Great Britain

1. ORIGINS OF THE SQUALL

1. Richard Bickerton Pemell, Lord Lyons, to John Russell, April 21, 1863, Private Letter Books, RBI, Lyons Papers, Arundel Castle, Sussex.

2. United States Navy Department, *Official Records of the Union and Confederate Navies in the War of the Rebellion* (29 vols., Washington, D.C., 1894–1922), Ser. 1, IV, 156; V, 625. Hereafter cited as *ORN*.

3. Gideon Welles to William W. McKean, Louis M. Goldsborough, Samuel F. Du Pont, and David G. Farragut, January 23 and 25, 1862, Letters to Officers Commanding Squadrons or Vessels, I, 245, 250, Record Group 45, National Archives.

4. Francis Deák and Philip C. Jessup, *A Collection of Neutrality Laws, Regulations and Treaties of Various Countries* (2 vols., Washington, D.C., 1939), I, 162.

5. Sir Robert Phillimore, *Commentaries upon International Law* (4 vols., London, 1854–1861), III, 405–407; E. S. Roscoe, ed., *Reports of Prize Cases Determined in the High Court of Admiralty from 1754–1859* (2 vols., London, 1905), I, 60–63.

6. Quoted in E. D. Adams, *Great Britain and the American Civil War* (2 vols., London, 1925), I, 263.

7. Liverpool *Journal of Commerce*, October 18, 1862; Charleston *Courier*, October 23, 1863; A. Sellow Roberts, "High Prices and the Blockade in the Confederacy," *South Atlantic Quarterly*, XXIV (April, 1925), 159–160.

8. Richmond *Dispatch*, June 3, 1864; Vice Admiral David Dixon Porter, Private Journal No. 1, p. 823, Container 23, David Dixon Porter Papers, Library of Congress.

9. William Watson, *The Adventures of a Blockade Runner; or, Trade in Time of War* (London, 1892), p. 144.

10. James D. Bulloch, *The Secret Service of the Confederate States in Europe or How the Confederate Cruisers Were Equipped* (2 vols., New York, 1959), I, 81; Watson, *Adventures of a Blockade Runner*, p. 14; Francis B. C. Bradlee, *Blockade Running During the Civil War and the Effect of Land and Water Transportation on the Confederacy* (Salem, Massachusetts, 1925), p. 136; W. R. Hooper, "Blockade-running," *Harper's New Monthly Magazine*, XLII (December, 1870), 107.

11. Sister Mary M. O'Rourke, "The Diplomacy of William H. Seward During the Civil War: His Policies as Related to International Law," Ph.D. dissertation, University of California, Berkeley, 1963, pp. 105–106; Carlton Savage, *Policy of the United States Toward Maritime Commerce in War* (2 vols., Washington, D.C., 1934), I, 114–115

12. Thomas H. Stevens to Welles, April 14, 1863, *ORN*, Ser. 1, II, 156–157; Lyons to Seward, August 7, 1863, and Seward to Lyons, August 13, 1863, United States Department of State, *Diplomatic Correspondence, Papers Relating to Foreign Affairs* (239 vols., Washington, D.C., 1861–1969), 1862/63, I, 619, 622 (hereafter cited as *PRFA*); Lyons to Seward, November 2, 1863, Letters Received, State Department, box 5, 1862–1864, Attorney General Papers, Record Group 60, National Archives; Seward to Welles, November 4, 1863, United States Department of State, Domestic Letters of the Department of State, LXII, 215, Record Group 59, National Archives.

13. *ORN*, Ser. 1, IV, 363–364; V, 622; Horatio L. Wait, "The Blockade of the Confederacy," *Century Magazine* (July, 1898), 914;

Anonymous, "Blockade," *United States Naval Institute Proceedings*, XI (1885), 430.

14. "Instructions to officers commanding vessels attached to the Eastern Gulf Blockading Squadron," January 1, 1863, *ORN*, Ser. 1, XVII, 341; Madeline Robinton, *An Introduction to the Papers of the New York Prize Court, 1861–1865* (New York, 1945), p. 49.

15. Francis H. Upton, *The Law of Nations Affecting Commerce During War; with a Review of Jurisdiction, Practice and Proceedings of Prize Courts* (New York, 1863), pp. 395–396, 441–442; Robinton, *Papers of the New York Prize Court*, pp. 28, 30.

16. Robinton, *Papers of the New York Prize Court*, pp. 140–142.

17. William Atherton and Roundell Palmer to Russell, June 27, 1862, Great Britain, Foreign Office 83/2214. These papers, located in the Public Record Office in London, will hereafter be cited as FO.

18. John Bassett Moore, *A Digest of International Law* (8 vols., Washington, D.C., 1906), VII, 562; Frank L. Owsley, "America and Freedom of the Seas, 1861–65," in *Essays in Honor of William E. Dodd*, ed. Avery Craven (Chicago, 1935), p. 201; M. R. Pitt, "Great Britain and Belligerent Maritime Rights from the Declaration of Paris, 1856, to the Declaration of London, 1909," Ph.D. dissertation, University of London, 1964, pp. 38–41.

19. Pitt, "Great Britain and Belligerent Maritime Rights," pp. 44–45.

20. O'Rourke, "Diplomacy of William H. Seward," pp. 217, 220; Dexter Perkins, "William H. Seward as Secretary of State," in Union College, *Union Worthies Number Six, William H. Seward* (Schenectady, 1951), p. 12.

21. O'Rourke, "Diplomacy of William H. Seward," pp. 219–220.

22. Hooper, "Blockade-running," 108; Bradley S. Osbon, *Handbook of the U.S. Navy; Being a Compilation of Main Events of Every U.S. Naval Vessel, April, 1861–May 1864* (New York, 1864), pp. 223–224; John S. Barnes, "My Egotistigraphy: The Egotistigraphy of a Rolling Stone, that gathered Moss, herein scraped off for the information and amusement of his family," typescript copy, 1910, New York Historical Society Library, pp. 201–202, 205; *Daily National Intelligencer*, November 11, 1861; James P. Baxter, III, "The British Government and Neutral Rights, 1861–1865," *American Historical Review*, XXXIV (October, 1928), 20.

23. Welles to Seward, May 12, 1863, Letterbook LIV, Gideon Welles Papers, Library of Congress; "Remarks on the Difficulty of Enforcing the Blockade and its Violation by British Vessels," August,

1862, Gideon Welles Papers, Henry E. Huntington Library, San Marino, California; *The Diary of Gideon Welles,* ed. Howard K. Beale (3 vols., New York, 1960), I, 106–107, 133, 170; Edward Bates to Seward, October 20, 1864, United States Department of Justice, *Official Opinions of the Attorneys General of the United States* (41 vols., Washington, D.C., 1852–1960), XI, 118–119; Bates to Lincoln, February 9, 1863, *The Collected Works of Abraham Lincoln,* ed. Roy P. Basler (9 vols., New Brunswick, New Jersey, 1953), VI, 74; Russell to Stuart, September 18, 1863, P.R.O. 30/22/97.

24. Lyons to Russell, May 26, 1862, Great Britain, Parliament, "Correspondence Respecting Interference with Trade between New York and the Bahamas," North America, No. 14 (1863), p. 4.

25. William Stuart to Seward, June 1 and September 25, 1862, *ibid.,* pp. 19, 40–41.

26. Seward to Stuart, October 10, 1862, *ibid.,* pp. 48–49.

27. Russell to Lyons, December 17, 1862, and Seward to Lyons, January 9, 1863, *ibid.,* pp. 56–58.

28. Lyons to Seward, May 18, 1863, *ibid.,* p. 60; Lyons to Seward, October 30, 1863, January 6, February 9 and 19, April 13, May 27, 28, 29, June 27, 1864, Seward to Lyons, July 30, 1864, *PRFA,* 1864, II, 394–395, 469–470, 520–521, 524–528, 582–583, 617–618, 642.

29. Lyons to Seward, August 4, 1864, and Seward to Lyons, August 8, 1864, *PRFA,* 1864, II, 668 and 673.

2. COULD THERE BE A BLOCKADE? THE PRIZE CASES

1. Louis B. Boudin, *Government by Judiciary* (2 vols., New York, 1932), II, 38; David M. Silver, *Lincoln's Supreme Court* (Urbana, 1956), p. 104; Clinton L. Rossiter, *The Supreme Court and the Commander in Chief* (Ithaca, 1951), p. 68; Charles Warren, *The Supreme Court in the United States* (2 vols., Boston, 1926), II, 381.

2. Gideon Welles to The President, August 5, 1861, *ORN,* Ser. 1, VI, 53–56; William H. Seward to Charles F. Adams, June 8, 1861, United States Department of State, Diplomatic Instructions, Great Britain, 1801–1906, Microfilm Roll 76, XVI, Record Group 59, National Archives; Sister Mary M. O'Rourke, "The Diplomacy of William H. Seward During the Civil War," Ph.D. dissertation, University of California, Berkeley, 1963, pp. 96, 103.

3. Mountague Bernard, *A Historical Account of the Neutrality of Great Britain during the American Civil War* (London, 1870), p. 115; O'Rourke, "Diplomacy of William H. Seward," p. 54; James

G. Randall, *Constitutional Problems under Lincoln* (Urbana, 1951), p. 60.

4. John M. Zane, *Lincoln the Constitutional Lawyer* (Springfield, Illinois, 1933), pp. 84–87; George F. Milton, *The Use of Presidential Power, 1789–1943* (Boston, 1944), pp. 109–110.

5. United States, *Statutes at Large of the United States of America, from the organization of the government in 1789 to concurrent resolutions in the two houses of Congress and recent treaties, conventions, and executive proclamations* (39 vols., Boston and Washington, D.C., 1845–1919), XII, 255–257, 326; Boudin, *Government by Judiciary*, II, 38.

6. Richard H. Dana to Adams, March 9, 1863, and Thornton K. Lothrop to Adams, August 25, 1890, in Charles Francis Adams, *Richard Henry Dana: A Biography* (2 vols., Cambridge, 1890), II, 266, 398–399; Silver, *Lincoln's Supreme Court*, p. 106; Carl B. Swisher, *Roger B. Taney* (New York, 1935), pp. 563–564.

7. United States District Court, Massachusetts, *Decisions of Hon. Peleg Sprague, 1841–64,* ed. Richard Henry Dana (2 vols., Boston, 1868), II, 127–150; *U.S. Supreme Court Reports, Cases Argued and Decided in the Supreme Court of the United States,* Lawyers' Edition (118 vols., Rochester, 1917–1967), XVII, 460–461.

8. *U.S. Supreme Court Reports,* L.Ed., XVII, 460–461.

9. United States District Court of the Southern District of New York, *United States of America against the Hiawatha and Her Cargo. Argument of Mr. Charles Edwards, in the Case of the British Barque Hiawatha, as Advocate for Owners of the Vessel and portion of her Cargo, also for H. B. M.'s Consul at New York, intervening for absent British owners of other parts* (New York, 1861), pp. 5–39; Samuel R. Betts, *The Blockade: Opinion of Hon. Samuel R. Betts, Judge of the U.S. District Court for the Southern District of N.Y., in the cases of The Hiawatha and other vessels captured as prize* (New York, 1861), pp. 9–25; Samuel R. Betts to E. Delafield Smith, October 8, 1861, in Smith to Seward, October 9, 1861, United States Department of State, Miscellaneous Letters of the Department of State, Microfilm Roll 184, p. 135, Record Group 59, National Archives; *U.S. Supreme Court Reports,* L.Ed., XVII, 461.

10. John D. Harding to John Russell, July 5, 1861, FO 83/2211; Russell to Richard B. P. Lyons, September 21, 1861, FO 5/1178.

11. Harding to Russell, October 31, 1861, FO 83/2212; Harding to Russell, March 21, 1862, FO 83/2213; Russell to Lyons, March 27, 1862, FO 5/1178.

12. *U.S. Supreme Court Reports*, L.Ed., XVII, 460; *The Federal Cases, Comprising Cases Argued and Determined in the Circuit and District Courts of the United States* (30 vols., St. Paul, Minnesota, 1894–1897), XII, 104–108.

13. *U.S. Supreme Court Reports*, L.Ed., XVII, 460; Supreme Court of the United States, Case Number 231, Rafael Preciat, Claimant of the Mexican Schooner Brilliant and Cargo, Appellant, vs. The United States. Appeal from the District Court of the United States for the Southern District of Florida, in U.S. Supreme Court, Records and Briefs, 2 *Black* 613–672, Library of Congress Law Library.

14. William M. Evarts to Edward Bates, November 23, 1861, container 1, William M. Evarts Papers, Library of Congress; Miscellaneous correspondence relative to disposition of vessels and property captured by U.S. ships, 1861–1865, folder 4711, XZ Prizes, prize money, and prize sales (legal and financial aspects), Record Group 45, National Archives.

15. Bates to Evarts, March 11, 1862, Attorney General Papers, Letterbooks, B–5, p. 55, Record Group 60, National Archives; *The Diary of Edward Bates, 1859–1866*, ed. Howard K. Beale, *Annual Report of the American Historical Association for 1930* (Washington, D.C., 1933), IV, 231; Silver, *Lincoln's Supreme Court*, pp. 105–106; Samuel Shapiro, *Richard Henry Dana, Jr., 1815–1882* (East Lansing, Michigan, 1961), p. 120.

16. Shapiro, *Richard Henry Dana, Jr.*, p. 120; Silver, *Lincoln's Supreme Court*, pp. 107, 109–110.

17. *U.S. Supreme Court Reports*, L.Ed., XVII, 464, 474–476.

18. Shapiro, *Richard Henry Dana, Jr.*, p. 121.

19. *U.S. Supreme Court Reports*, L.Ed., XVII, 468–474.

20. Adams, *Richard Henry Dana*, p. 270; The Supreme Court of the United States, Mr. Sedgwick's Brief for the Captors (n.p., n.d.), pp. 5–17, in U.S. Supreme Court, Records and Briefs, 2 *Black* 613–672, Library of Congress Law Library; *Arguments and Speeches of William Maxwell Evarts*, ed. Sherman Evarts (3 vols., New York, 1919), I, 214–294; Edward Bates, *Diary*, 281.

21. New York *World*, March 11, 1863.

22. Samuel F. Miller, *Reports of Decisions in the Supreme Court of the United States* (4 vols., Washington, D.C., 1874–1875), IV, 878–906.

23. Swisher, *Roger B. Taney*, pp. 565–566; Carl B. Swisher, *Stephen J. Field: Craftsman of the Law* (Washington, D.C., 1930), p. 115; Silver, *Lincoln's Supreme Court*, pp. 84–85, 87–88.

24. Boudin, *Government by Judiciary*, II, 43–44; Swisher, *Roger B. Taney*, pp. 566–572; Rossiter, *Supreme Court*, pp. 75–76; Charles G. Haines and Foster H. Sherwood, *The Role of the Supreme Court in American Government and Politics, 1835–1864* (2 vols., Berkeley, 1957), II, 477.

25. Rossiter, *The Supreme Court and the Commander in Chief*, p. 71; Randall, *Constitutional Problems under Lincoln*, p. 313; Lyons to Russell, November 11, 1863, FO 5/1178.

3. THE LABUAN: FIRST OF THE MATAMOROS CASES

1. Corpus Christi *Nueces Valley*, January 23, 1858, quoted in Leroy P. Graf, "The Economic History of the Lower Rio Grande Valley, 1820–1875," Ph.D. dissertation, 2 vols., Harvard University, 1942, II, p. 489; Gideon Welles to Salmon P. Chase, April 21, 1863, *ORN*, Ser. 1, XVII, 417; Raphael Semmes, *Memoirs of Service Afloat During the War Between the States* (Baltimore, 1869), pp. 792–793.

2. Leonard Pierce, Jr., to William H. Seward, March 1, 1862, United States Department of the Army, *The War of the Rebellion: A Compilation of the Official Records of the Union and Confederate Armies* (128 vols., Washington, D.C., 1880–1901), Series 1, IX, 675, to be cited as *OR*, Pierce to Samuel Swartwout, March 7, 1862, *ORN*, Ser. 1, XVIII, 54; Juan A. Quintero to William M. Browne, March 22 and 28, and Quintero to Judah P. Benjamin, August 14, 1862, box 8, folder 80; Quintero to Benjamin, November 2, 1862, folder 81; Quintero to Benjamin, November 5, 1864, folder 84, Confederate States of America, State Department Records, Library of Congress; Robert W. Delaney, "Matamoros, Port for Texas during the Civil War," *Southwestern Historical Quarterly*, LVIII (April, 1955), 478–479; Herbert Davenport, "Notes on Early Steamboating on the Rio Grande," *Southwestern Historical Quarterly*, XLIX (October, 1945), 289; Laura Snyder, "The Blockade of the Texas Coast During the Civil War," M.A. thesis, Texas Technological College, 1938, pp. 93–94.

3. Charles W. Ramsdell, "The Texas State Military Board, 1862–1865," *Southwestern Historical Quarterly*, LVIII (April, 1955), 254, 266; Bonnye R. Whitworth, "The Role of Texas in the Confederacy," M.A. thesis, North Texas State College, 1951, p. 101; Delaney, "Matamoros," 479.

4. Welles to Chase, April 21, 1863, *ORN*, Ser. 1, XVII, 417; Tom Lea, *The King Ranch* (2 vols., Boston, 1957), I, 192.

5. *Treaties and Other International Acts of the United States of America*, ed. Hunter Miller (8 vols., Washington, D.C., 1937), V,

216–217; Harold R. Pyke, *The Law of Contraband of War* (London, 1915), p. 155; *ORN*, Ser. 1, IV, 156; V, 625.

6. McKean to Swartwout, January 17, 1862, and Swartwout to McKean, February 3, 1862, *ORN*, Ser. 1, XVII, 101–103.

7. Richard B. P. Lyons to Seward, March 8, 1862, Notes from the British Legation, XLIII; Louis Blacker to Joseph T. Crawford, February 9, 1862, *ORN,* Ser. 1, XVII, 109–111.

8. Edward Tatham to Swartwout, March 18, 1862, *ORN*, Ser. 1, XVII, 82; Graf, "Lower Rio Grande Valley," II, 535; Robin W. Winks, *Canada and the United States: The Civil War Years* (Baltimore, 1960), p. 126; Crawford to Russell, March 1, 1862, FO 97/42.

9. Seward to Lyons, March 8, 1862, United States Department of State, Notes from the Department of State to foreign ministers and consuls in the United States, Great Britain, 1834–1906, Microfilm Roll 38, pp. 135–136, Record Group 59, National Archives; Seward to Welles, March 13, 1862, Domestic Letters, LVI, 487; Welles to Farragut, March 14, 1862, *ORN*, Ser. 1, XVIII, 66.

10. Seward to Lyons, March 13, and April 6, 1862, Notes from the Department of State, Roll 38, pp. 137, 165; Pierce to Seward, March 21, 1862, United States Department of State, Consular Despatches, Matamoros, Roll 3, Record Group 59, National Archives.

11. Edmund Hammond to Admiralty, March 25, 1862, FO 97/42; William G. Romaine to Milne, March 28, April 6, 1862, Admiralty 128/58, Public Record Office (hereafter cited as Adm.).

12. Alexander Milne to Tatham, September 13, 1862, Milne/103/18 (R), Milne Papers, National Maritime Museum, Greenwich (hereafter cited as MLN/); Dunlop to Admiralty, November 24, 1862, MLN/104/3; Hancock to Hugh Dunlop, March 2, 1863, MLN/104/4; Milne to Maguire, December 22, 1863, FO 5/1181; Harding, William Atherton, and Roundell Palmer to Russell, April 3, 1862, FO 83/2213; Palmer, Robert P. Collier, Robert J. Phillimore to Russell, January 30, 1864, FO 83/2220.

13. Lyons to Seward, April 23, 1862, United States Department of State, Notes from the British Legation in the United States to the Department of State, 1791–1906, XLIV, Record Group 59, National Archives.

14. Seward to Lyons, April 26, 1862, Notes from the Department of State, Roll 38, pp. 165–166; Seward to E. Delafield Smith, April 26, 1862, Domestic Letters, LVII, 129; Smith to Seward, May 26, 1862, Miscellaneous Letters, Roll 190, p. 806.

15. Seward to Edwin M. Stanton, January 29, March 13, and July 18, 1862, Domestic Letters, LVI, 259, 488; LVII, 124, 499; Peter H. Watson to Seward, February 3, March 19 and 24, 1862, *OR*, Ser. 1, IX, 629, 650, 655.

16. J. Bankhead Magruder to William R. Boggs, November 10, 1863; James H. Strong to Henry H. Bell, November 10 and December 28, 1863, *ORN*, Ser. 1, XX, 650, 667, 742; Nannie M. Tillie, *Federals on the Frontier; The Diary of Benjamin F. McIntyre, 1862–1864* (Austin, 1963), p. 255; Charles I. Evans, "Military Events and Operations in Texas and Along the Coasts and Border, 1861–1865," in *A Comprehensive History of Texas,* ed. Dudley G. Wooten (2 vols., Dallas, 1898), II, 539; Whitworth, "Role of Texas in the Confederacy," p. 102.

17. Hamilton P. Bee to Quintero, November 9, 1863, Peter Kinney to Seward, May 21, 1864, James H. Fry to W. G. Tobin, August 4, 1864, Theodore H. Barrett to Lorenzo Thomas, August 10, 1865, *OR*, Ser. 1, XXVI, Part 2, pp. 399–400; XXIV, Part 4, p. 467; XLI, Part 1, pp. 185–186; XLVIII, Part 1, 265–267; Seward to Welles, August 14, 1864, *ORN*, Ser. 1, XXI, 605; Delaney, "Matamoros," 486; Orville E. Avery, "Confederate Defense of Texas, 1861–1865," M.A. thesis, University of Oklahoma, 1940, pp. 94–95, 113; Charles W. Ramsdell, "Texas in the Confederacy," *The History of the Southern States,* pp. 413–414, in *The South in the Building of the Nation* (12 vols., Richmond, Virginia, 1909), III; Anonymous, "The Last Battle of the War," *Southern Historical Society Papers,* XXI (1893), 226–227.

18. William Stuart to Seward, October 12, 1862, Notes from the British Legation, XLVI; Seward to Smith, October 16, 1862, Domestic Letters, LVIII, 355.

19. Lyons to Seward, March 28, 1863, Notes from the British Legation, XLIX; Seward to Lyons, April 9, 1863, Notes from the Department of State, Roll 38, pp. 538–542.

20. Seward to Smith, April 13 and 18, 1863, Seward to Welles, May 8, 1863, Domestic Letters, LX, 218, 262–263, 378; Smith to Seward, April 17, 1863, Miscellaneous Letters, Roll 190, pp. 490–491.

21. Stuart to Seward, September 24, 1863, Lyons to Seward, November 21 and December 19, 1863, March 2 and August 5, 1864, Notes from the British Legation, LV, LVI, LVII, LX, LXVII; J. Hume Burnley to Seward, December 9, 1864, *PRFA*, 1865, II, 6–7; Seward to Stuart, September 30, 1863, Seward to Lyons, November 25, 1863, March 3, July 8, August 15, 1864, Seward to Burnley, January 18, 1865, Notes from the Department of State, Roll 39, pp. 283,

313–314, Roll 40, pp. 30, 435, Roll 41, pp. 7–8, Roll 42, pp. 17–18.

22. United States District Court, Southern District of New York, Case Number 71, The Steamer *Labuan*, 71–50, 71–53, 71–54, on microfilm at Columbia University; Smith to Seward, December 14, 1864, Miscellaneous Letters, Roll 219, pp. 462–464.

23. Edward Thornton to Seward, April 4, 1868, Notes from the British Legation, LXXXVI; Seward to Charles Sumner, April 13, 1868, United States Congress, Senate, *Congressional Globe* (46 vols., Washington, D.C., 1833–1873), 41st Congress, 2nd session, 1869–70, Part 4, p. 2892.

24. *Congressional Globe*, 40th Congress, 3rd session, 1868–69, Part 3, p. 153; 41st Congress, 1869–70, Part 4, pp. 3316, 5252, 5300, 5319, 5375.

25. Hiram Barney to Edward M. Archibald, November 7 and 8, 1862, Notes from the British Legation, XLVI.

26. "Report of Robert S. Hale, Esq., Agent and Counsel of the United States Before the Commission on Claims of Citizens of the United States against Great Britain, and of Subjects of Her Britannic Majesty against the United States, under the Twelfth Article of the Treaty of 8th May, 1871, between the United States and Great Britain," *PRFA*, 1873, III, 208.

4. The Matamoros Cases: The Union Persists

1. Charles Hunter to Gideon Welles, June 3, 1862, *ORN*, Ser. 1, XVIII, 525–526; Louis Blacker to Frederick Jonson, June 9, 1862, "Correspondence Respecting the Seizure of the British Schooner 'Will o'The Wisp' by the United States' Ship of War 'Montgomery,' at Matamoros, June 3, 1862," Great Britain, House of Commons, *Sessional Papers*, LXXII, 1863, North America, No. 12, pp. 1–2.

2. Edward Tatham to David G. Farragut, June 16, 1862, in "Correspondence Respecting the 'Will o' The Wisp,' " p. 4; William Stuart to John Russell, July 21, 1862, Public Record Office 30/36/1 (hereafter cited as P.R.O.); Stuart to Alexander Milne, July 21, 1862, Adm. 128/59; Stuart to William H. Seward, July 19, 1862, Adm. 128/59; Seward to Stuart, July 23, 1862, Notes from the Department of State, Roll 38, p. 228.

3. Thomas J. Boynton to Seward, August 9, 1862, Notes from the Department of State, Roll 38, pp. 10–11.

4. Stuart to Seward, October 20, 1862, *ibid.*, pp. 14–15; Phillimore to Russell, September 15, 1862, FO 83/2214; Seward to Richard B. P. Lyons, December 22, 1862, *PRFA*, 1862/63, I, 422.

5. Lyons to Seward, March 17, 1863, and Seward to Lyons, April 2, 1863, *PRFA*, 1862/63, I, 467–468, 478–479.

6. "Report of Robert S. Hale, Esq.," *PRFA*, 1873, III, 92.

7. T. Frederick Elliot to Edmund Hammond, April 18, 1863, in "Correspondence Respecting 'Will o' The Wisp,'" pp. 43–46; Seward to Lyons, January 28, 1864, *PRFA*, 1864, II, 508; Stephen R. Mallory to James D. Bulloch, September 20, 1864, *ORN*, Ser. 2, II, 726; Robin W. Winks, *Canada and the United States: The Civil War Years* (Baltimore, 1960), pp. 126–127.

8. J. Frederick Nickels to Welles, January 28, 1863, and Boynton to Welles, February 28, 1863, *ORN*, Ser. 1, II, 62–63; Protest of Robert A. Stanbury, William H. Tamlin, and Henry Thompson, February 26, 1863, and Aubrey G. Butterfield to Archibald, March 6, 1863, FO 5/1180.

9. Lyons to Seward, April 22, 1863, *PRFA*, 1862/63, I, 511.

10. Welles to Seward, May 23, 1863, Miscellaneous Letters, Roll 200, pp. 421–422; Seward to William M. Evarts, November 16, 1863, Container 1, p. 48, William M. Evarts Papers, Library of Congress; Thornton to Clarendon, August 30, 1869, FO 5/1180.

11. Henry H. Bell to Welles, September 17, 1863, Henry Rolando to Welles, September 11, 1863, Rolando to Gustavus V. Fox, October 3, 1863, *ORN*, Ser. 1, XX, 567–569, 579–580.

12. Lyons to Seward, November 2, 1863, Notes from the British Legation, LVI; Seward to Lyons, November 5, 1863, Notes from the Department of State, Roll 39, p. 334; Russell to Lyons, December 7, 1863, FO 5/1181.

13. Charles H. Brown to Welles, November 6, 1863, and Edmund W. Henry to Welles, November 5, 1863, *ORN*, Ser. 1, XX, 658–659; John Read to John Angel, November 24, 1863, FO 5/1181.

14. Roundell Palmer, Robert P. Collier, Robert J. Phillimore to Russell, January 12, 1864, FO 83/2220.

15. Milne to Bell, December 23, 1863, FO 5/1181; Lyons to Seward, January 8, 1864, Notes from the British Legation, LVIII.

16. Welles to William W. McKean, November 25, 1861, Gideon Welles Papers, New York Public Library; Farragut to Hunter, April 16, 1862, *ORN*, Ser. 1, XVIII, 130.

17. Stuart to Russell, August 8, 1862, PRO 30/36/10; Seward to Welles, August 8, 1862, Domestic Letters, LVIII, 35–36; Farragut to Henry French, August 5, 1862, and Welles to flag-officers commanding squadrons and officers commanding cruisers, relative to the right of search, August 18, 1862, *ORN*, Ser. 1, XIX, 168, I, 417–418; *The*

Diary of Gideon Welles, ed. Howard K. Beale (3 vols., New York, 1960), I, 79–80.

18. Instructions to U.S. Cruizers in Matamoros Waters, August 8, 1863, FO 5/1181.

19. Milne to Admiralty, January 8, 1864, and Russell to Lyons, February 5, 1864, FO 5/1182; Lyons to Seward, March 1, 1864, *PRFA,* 1864, II, 536.

20. Lyons to Seward, March 1, 1864, Notes from the British Legation, LX.

21. Seward to Lyons, March 9, 1864, enclosing Welles to Seward, March 5, 1864, *PRFA,* 1864, II, 547–548.

22. Palmer, Collier, and Phillimore to Russell, April 26, 1864, FO 83/2221.

23. United States vs. Schooner Matamoros and Cargo, No. 7767, Reasons for Judgment, FO 5/1183; George Coppell to Lyons, June 6, 15, 1864, Coppell to Russell, June 16, August 27, 1864, FO 5/1183; Rufus Waples to Seward, November 2, 1864, in Seward to Lyons, November 21, 1864, *PRFA,* 1863/64, II, 784–785; J. Sceales to Lyons, July 1, 1864, FO 5/1183.

24. J. Hume Burnley to Seward, October 6, 1864, *PRFA,* 1863/64, II, 733–734; Coppell to Burnley, October 14, 1864, FO 5/1184.

25. Seward to Burnley, October 25, 1864, *PRFA,* 1863/64, II, 752; Bates to Seward, October 20, 1864, United States Department of Justice, *Official Opinions of the Attorney Generals,* XI, 117; Lyons to Seward, July 11, 1864, FO 5/1183; Hammond to Messrs. Deane & Co., June 15, 1865, FO 5/1184.

26. *U.S. Supreme Court Reports,* L.Ed., XVIII, 699.

27. *Ibid.,* 624–625.

28. *Ibid.,* 625–626.

29. *Ibid.,* 626.

30. Frederick W. A. Bruce to Edward H. Stanley, July 9, 1867 and June 11, 1870, Edward Thornton to Stanley, October 3, 1868, Thornton to Richard Grenville, October 24, 1870, Thornton to Grenville, January 30, 1871, FO 5/1185.

31. "Report of Robert S. Hale, Esq.," *PRFA,* 1873, III, 103–113.

32. *Ibid.,* 110–114; Mixed Commission on British and American Claims, *List of Claims of British Subjects Against the United States, and American Citizens Against Great Britain, Before the Mixed Commission Under the Twelfth Article of the Treaty of Washington of May 8, 1871* (Washington, D.C., 1873), pp. 30–31, 36–37, 48–51.

5. The Peterhoff: A Case of Continuous Voyage

1. Freeman H. Morse to William H. Seward, November 28 and December 19, 1862, United States Department of State, Despatches from United States Consuls in London, England, 1790–1906, XXX, Record Group 59, National Archives; John W. Wallace, *Cases Argued and Adjudged in the Supreme Court of the United States, 1863–1874* (23 vols., Washington, 1870–1876), V, 31–32.

2. United States District Court, Southern District of New York, *The United States v. The Steamer Peterhoff and Her Cargo, in Prize, Opinion of the Court, by Judge Betts* (New York, 1864), p. 11 (cited hereafter as *U.S. v. Steamer Peterhoff*); Richard B. P. Lyons to Seward, April 8, 1863, *PRFA*, 1862/63, I, 491; Wallace, *Cases in the Supreme Court*, V, 31–32.

3. Wallace, *Cases in the Supreme Court*, V, 32; Henry Adams to Charles Francis Adams, Jr., November 30, 1861, *A Cycle of Adams Letters, 1861–1865*, ed. Worthington C. Ford (2 vols., Boston, 1920), I, 76; Autobiography of Charles Wilkes, p. 2357, Charles Wilkes Papers, Library of Congress.

4. Wallace, *Cases in the Supreme Court*, V, 32–34; Frederick Mohl to Judah P. Benjamin, April 20, 1863, *ORN*, Ser. 1, II, 101; Alexander Milne to Lyons, March 23, 1863, Notes from the British Legation, L; *The British Steam-Ship "Peterhoff," A Report of Her Seizure by the United States Prize Court, at New York, Before the Hon. Judge Betts* (New York, 1863), Appendix, xi. This will be cited as *Peterhoff Seizure*.

5. Harold R. Pyke, *The Law of Contraband of War* (London, 1915), p. 155.

6. "Instructions of the Secretary of the Navy to flag-officers commanding squadrons and officers commanding cruisers, relative to the right of search. August 18, 1862." *ORN*, Ser. 1, I, 417–418; Charles B. Elliott, "The Doctrine of Continuous Voyages," *American Journal of International Law*, I (January, 1907), 96; Julius W. Pratt, "The British Blockade and American Precedents," *United States Naval Institute Proceedings*, XLVI (November, 1920), 1790.

7. Charles C. Hyde, *International Law Chiefly as Interpreted and Applied by the United States* (3 vols., Boston, 1945, III, 2131; Carlton Savage, *Policy of the United States Toward Maritime Commerce in War* (2 vols., Washington, D.C., 1934), I, 117–118, 132–133; Joseph M. Kenworthy and George Young, *Freedom of the Seas* (New York, 1928), p. 31.

8. *Harper's Weekly*, April 25, 1863; Mason to Benjamin, March 30, 1863, *A Compilation of the Messages and Papers of The Confederacy*, ed. James D. Richardson (2 vols., Nashville, 1906), II, 468.

9. "American Seizures of English Ships," *Saturday Review*, XV (April 23, 1863), 516; *Observer*, April 19, 1863; *The Times* (London), April 2, 16, 1863.

10. *Hansard's* (3rd Series, 356 vols., London 1830–1891), CLXX, 72–81, 577, 600; Wilbur D. Jones, "The British Conservatives and the American Civil War," *American Historical Review*, LVIII (April, 1953), 528; *The Dictionary of National Biography*, ed. Sir Leslie Stephen and Sir Sidney Lee (22 vols., London, 1921–1922), XVII, 96–97; Frank L. Owsley, *King Cotton Diplomacy* (Chicago, 1931), p. 475; *The Times*, January 5, 1882.

11. *The Times*, April 7, 1863.

12. *New York Times*, April 20, 1863; James P. Baxter, III, "Some British Opinions as to Neutral Rights, 1861 to 1865," *American Journal of International Law*, XXIII (July, 1929), 517.

13. Lyons to John Russell, May 5, 1863; FO 5/937; Seward to Lyons, April 15, 1863, *PRFA*, 1862/63, I, 507.

14. Lyons to Seward, May 6 and 7, 1863, *PRFA*, 1862/63, I, 524–525, 534–535.

15. Seward to Lyons, May 7 and 12, 1863, *PRFA*, I, 536–537, 540; *Diary of Gideon Welles*, ed. Howard K. Beale (3 vols., New York, 1960), I, 299; Seward to Adams, May 12, 1863, Diplomatic Instructions, XVIII, 490; London *Morning Post*, March 27, 1863; *The Times*, April 16 and 21, 1863; "Belligerents and Neutrals," *Saturday Review*, XV (May 2, 1863), 545; Douglas Maynard, "The Forbes-Aspinwall Mission," *Mississippi Valley Historical Review*, XLV (June, 1958), 73, 81; *Letters and Recollections of John Murray Forbes*, ed. Sarah F. Hughes (2 vols., Boston, 1899), II, 45.

16. Lyons to Seward, April 9 and 13, 1863, *PRFA*, 1862/63, I, 496–497, 505–506; Seward to E. Delafield Smith, April 12, 1863, Domestic Letters, LX, 230.

17. James P. Baxter, III, "The British Government and Neutral Rights, 1861–1865," *American Historical Review*, XXXIV (October, 1928), 9; James P. Baxter, III, "Papers Relating to Belligerent and Neutral Rights, 1861–1865," *American Historical Review*, XXXIV (October, 1928), 87; John Bassett Moore, *A Digest of International Law* (8 vols., Washington, D.C., 1906), VII, 482–483; Welles, *Diary*, I, 269–270; Gideon Welles, *Lincoln and Seward* (New York, 1874), pp. 93–96; Welles to the President, April 25, 1863, "U.S. vs. The

British Steamer 'Peterhoff.' Contem. Cops. of Letters on the Above Case from William H. Seward, Gideon Welles, A. Lincoln, Francis H. Upton, C. H. Baldwin, Chas. Wilkes & Others," pp. 1–21, Gideon Welles Papers, Henry E. Huntington Memorial Library.

18. *The Collected Works of Abraham Lincoln,* ed. Roy P. Basler (9 vols., New Brunswick, New Jersey, 1953), VI, 183; Welles, *Diary,* I, 286, 287; Seward to Lyons, April 17, 1863, *PRFA,* 1862/63, I, 510; United States District Court, Southern District of New York, Prize Court Papers, The Steamer *Peterhoff,* Case Number 151, Papers #14. This group of documents, available on microfilm at Columbia University, is cited hereafter as Peterhoff Papers. Seward to Welles, May 21, 1863, Domestic Letters, LX, 475; Lyons to Russell, May (n.d.), 1863, Notes from the British Legation, LI.

19. *New York Times,* April 23, 1863; Boston *Daily Evening Transcript,* April 24, 1863; New York *Tribune,* April 25, 1863; London *Shipping and Mercantile Gazette, Daily News,* and *Globe,* quoted in *New York Times,* May 17, 1863; Welles, *Lincoln and Seward,* pp. 85–122. Seward had recently died and Charles Francis Adams paid his respects by means of *An Address on the Life, Character and Services of William Henry Seward* (Albany, 1873). This, to Welles, gave a slanted picture. The former Secretary of the Navy wrote his book so that "History would know The Truth."

20. Russell to Lyons, June 6, 1863, PRO 30/22/97; Printed Confidential Despatch from Lord Russell to Lyons, June 15, 1863, Printed for the use of the Cabinet, Palmerston Papers, National Register of Archives, London. By permission of the Trustees of the Broadlands Archives.

21. Charles F. Adams to Seward, April 18, 1863, Despatches from United States Ministers to Great Britain, 1791–1906, Microfilm Roll 78, Record Group 59, National Archives.

22. *The Times,* April 18, 1863; London *Index,* April 23, 1863, contains *Morning Herald* quote; *New York Times,* May 4, 1863.

23. *Hansard's,* 3rd Ser., CLXX, 559, 562; Adams to Seward, April 24, 1863, Despatches, Roll 78.

24. Lyons to Seward, May 7, 1863, Notes from the British Legation, LI; William L. Dayton to Seward, April 24, 1863, *PRFA,* 1862/63, I, 659–660; Seward to Lyons, May 8, 1863, Notes from the Department of State, Roll 39, pp. 2–3; Seward to Dayton, May 8, 1863, *PRFA,* 1862/63, I, 667.

25. Charles Francis Adams, Diary, May 27, 1863, Microfilm Roll 77, from the microfilms of The Adams Papers, owned by the Adams Manuscript Trust and deposited in the Massachusetts Historical

Society; *The Journal of Benjamin Moran, 1857–1865,* ed. Sarah A. Wallace and Frances E. Gillespie (2 vols., Chicago, 1948–1949), II, 1148; Martin B. Duberman, *Charles Francis Adams, 1807–1886* (Boston, 1960), pp. 307–308.

26. *Peterhoff Seizure,* pp. 262–263.

27. *Hansard's,* 3rd Ser., CLXX, 1831–1833; "Belligerents and Neutrals," 549–550; "American Prize Courts," *Saturday Review,* XV (May 23, 1863), 649; *The Times,* May 4 and June 30, 1863; Dudley to Seward, May 8, 1863, United States Department of State, Despatches from United States Consuls in Liverpool, England, 1790–1906, XXIII, Record Group 59, National Archives.

28. *Shipping and Mercantile Gazette* editorial reproduced in *New York Times,* September 7, 1863; *The Times,* August 19 and 20, 1863; Philadelphia *Public Ledger,* August 3, 1863; *Daily National Intelligencer,* August 5, 1863; *New York Times,* March 19, 1864.

29. Russell to Lyons, October 31, 1863, "Correspondence Respecting the 'Springbok' and 'Peterhoff' by United States cruisers in 1863," Great Britain, House of Commons, *Sessional Papers,* CV, 1900 (Cd. 34), p. 60.

30. *U.S. v. Steamer Peterhoff,* 54–55, 67, 69, 75–76, 78, 80–83, 91–93, 95, 98–104.

31. Russell to Lyons, April 22, 1864, "Correspondence Respecting the 'Springbok' and 'Peterhoff,' " p. 68.

32. Lyons to Seward, August 12, 1863, and Seward to Lyons, August 19, 1863, *PRFA,* 1862/63, I, 620, 624.

33. Wallace, *Cases in the Supreme Court,* V, 35, 49–62.

34. United States Department of State, *Papers Relating to the Treaty of Washington* (6 vols., Washington, 1874), VI, 137–139; Llewellyn A. Atherly-Jones, *Commerce in War* (London, 1907), p. 265; Ludwig Gessner, *Zur Reform des Kriegs-Seerechts* (Berlin, 1875), pp. 28–29, cited in Herbert W. Briggs, *The Doctrine of Continuous Voyage* (Baltimore, 1926), p. 68.

35. James W. Gantenbein, *The Doctrine of Continuous Voyage, Particularly as Applied to Contraband and Blockade* (Portland, Oregon, 1929), pp. 71–73.

36. *Ibid.,* pp. 69 and 85; Briggs, *Doctrine of Continuous Voyage,* p. 57; Norman Bentwich, *The Law of Private Property in War* (London, 1907), p. 113; Anonymous, "The Law of Ulterior Destination as Bearing on Contraband of War," *Law Magazine and Review,* XXX (1870), 86–87.

6. The Springbok: A Case of Continuous Voyage

1. Thomas H. Stevens to Gideon Welles, February 3, 1863, *ORN*, Ser. 1, II, 73; *The Federal Cases, Comprising Cases Argued and Determined in the Circuit and District Courts of the United States* (30 vols., St. Paul, Minnesota, 1894–1897), XXII, 995–998.

2. *The Federal Cases*, XXII, 997–1007.

3. John Russell to Richard B. P. Lyons, December 29, 1863, FO 5/994; Roundell Palmer, Robert P. Collier, Robert J. Phillimore to Russell, February 19, 1864, FO 83/2220; Russell to Lyons, February 20, 1864, "Correspondence Respecting the seizure of the British vessels 'Springbok' and 'Peterhoff' by United States cruisers in 1863," Great Britain, House of Commons, *Sessional Papers*, CV, 1900 (Cd. 34), pp. 39–40.

4. *Mémorial Diplomatique*, December 20, 1863, and March 27, 1864; translation into English of *Norddeutsche Allgemeine Zeitung*, February 1, 1866, in London *Globe*, March 5, 1866.

5. Palmer, Collier, and Phillimore to Russell, May 16, 1864, FO 83/2221.

6. *Shipping and Mercantile Gazette*, August 5, 1862; March 7 and 10, May 13, August 17 and 25, 1863.

7. *Globe*, December 4, 5, and 7, 1863; London *Observer*, December 6 and 20, 1863; *Morning Herald*, December 24, 1863; *Standard*, December 24, 1863, and March 10, 1866; London *Morning Advertiser*, January 2, 1864.

8. John W. Wallace, *Cases Argued and Adjudged in the Supreme Court, 1863–1874* (23 vols., Washington, D.C., 1870–1876), V, 20–28.

9. John Bassett Moore, *A Digest of International Law* (8 vols., Washington, D.C., 1906), VII, 731–732.

10. Sir Travers Twiss, "The Doctrine of Continuous Voyages as applied to Contraband of War and Blockade, contrasted with the Declaration of Paris of 1856," in *Prize Law and Continuous Voyage*, ed. Thomas Baty (London, 1915), pp. 17–18, 29, 30.

11. Louis Gessner, *A Juridicial Review of the Case of the British Barque "Springbok"* (London, 1875), pp. 22–23, 24, 35.

12. D.C.L., "Analysis of 'Springbok' Judgment," in *Prize Law and Continuous Voyage*, pp. 95, 105, 111, 112; Paul Fauchille, "La Théorie du Voyage Continu en Matière de Contrebande de Guerre," *Revue Générale de Droit Inter-national Public*, IV (1897), 304.

13. John B. Karslake, William B. Brett, and Travers Twiss to Stanley, July 29, 1867, FO 83/2225; E. C. Egerton to Forbes Camp-

bell, July 24, 1868, "Correspondence Respecting the 'Springbok' and 'Peterhoff,'" CV, 55–58.

14. Brainerd Dyer, *The Public Career of William M. Evarts* (Berkeley, 1933), pp. 149–150; "Report of Robert S. Hale, Esq.," *PRFA*, 1873, III, 122.

15. Moore, *Digest of International Law*, VII, 729; M. R. Pitt, "Great Britain and Belligerent Maritime Rights from the Declaration of Paris, 1856, to the Declaration of London, 1909," Ph.D. dissertation, University of London, 1964, p. 56.

16. Hamilton Cochran, *Blockade Runners of the Confederacy* (Indianapolis, 1958), pp. 33–34; James M. Merrill, *The Rebel Shore* (Boston, 1957), p. 64; Paul Hendren, "The Confederate Blockade Runners," *United States Naval Institute Proceedings*, LIX (April, 1933), 508.

17. Alexander Holtzoff, "Some Phases of the Law of Blockade," *American Journal of International Law*, X (January, 1916), 61–62; Charles N. Gregory, "The Doctrine of Continuous Voyage," *Harvard Law Review*, XXIV (January, 1911), 174; Herbert W. Briggs, *The Doctrine of Continuous Voyage* (Baltimore, 1926), p. 62.

18. Moore, *Digest of International Law*, VII, 729; Pitt, "Great Britain and Belligerent Maritime Rights," p. 45.

19. Thomas Baty, "Continuous Voyage as applied to Blockade and Contraband," *Transaction of The Grotius Society: Problems of Peace and War*, XX (London, 1935), 155; Holtzoff, "Some Phases of the Law of Blockade," 61–62.

7. THE VIOLATION OF NEUTRAL TERRITORY

1. Gideon Welles to James L. Lardner, June 10, 1862, and Lardner to Welles, July 9, 1862, *ORN*, Ser. 1, XVII, 263, 286.

2. Protest of R. N. Smith, William Scrimgeour, and August Lawrence, October 10, 1862, *ORN*, Ser. 1, XIX, 279–281.

3. John V. Crawford to William Stuart, October 13, 1862, and Stuart to Alexander Milne, October 27, 1862, Adm. 128/58; Robert W. Shufeldt to William H. Seward, October 9 and 12, 1862, United States Department of State, Despatches from United States Consuls in Havana, Microfilm Roll 45, Record Group 59, National Archives; Charles Wilkes to Welles, October 13, 1862, *ORN*, Ser. 1, I, 505; Seward to Gustave Koerner, October 21, 1862, United States Department of State, Diplomatic Instructions, Spain, Microfilm Roll 143, p. 363, Record Group 59, National Archives.

4. Horatio J. Perry to Seward, November 4, 1862, United States

Department of State, Despatches from United States Ministers to Spain, XLIV, Microfilm Roll 43, Record Group 59, National Archives.

5. *Ibid.;* Koerner to Seward, November 6, 1862, *ibid.; Memoirs of Gustave Koerner, 1809–1896,* ed. Thomas J. McCormack (2 vols., Cedar Rapids, 1909), II, 264–269.

6. Gabriel G. Tassara to Seward, October 20, 1862, and Seward to Tassara, October 23, 1862, *PRFA,* 1861/62, pp. 532–534, 537; Welles to Seward, October 27, 1862, Miscellaneous Letters, Roll 193, p. 404.

7. Tassara to Seward, December 4, 1862, United States Department of State, *Correspondence relative to the Steamer General Rusk, alias Blanche. To which is appended the proceedings of a court martial in the case of Commander Hunter* (Washington, 1863), pp. 193–195.

8. Seward to Tassara, December 6 and 17, 1862, *ibid.,* pp. 197, 200–201.

9. *The Times* (London), November 12, 1862; *Shipping and Mercantile Gazette,* November 4, 1862; *Manchester Guardian,* November 7, 1862; Stuart to Russell, October 21, 1862, PRO 30/22/36; William Atherton, Roundell Palmer, Robert J. Phillimore to John Russell, November 24, 1862, FO 83/2215.

10. Richard B. P. Lyons to Seward, December 9, 1862, Notes from the British Legation, XLV; Seward to Lyons, December 10, 1862, and Lyons to Seward, January 8, 1863, *PRFA,* 1862/63, I, 418–419, 432; Seward to Lyons, January 10, 1863, Notes from the Department of State, Roll 38, p. 402.

11. General Court Martial No. 3179, Records of the Office of the Judge Advocate General (Navy), Records of the General Courts-Martial and Courts of Inquiry, 1799–1867, Microfilm Roll 102, pp. 1272–1279, 1283–1284, Record Group 125, National Archives; Welles to the President, February 27, 1863, Letterbook LXXIII, 153, Gideon Welles Papers, Library of Congress; Albert Gleaves, "The Affair of the Blanche," *United States Naval Institute Proceedings,* XLVIII (October, 1922), 1673, 1676; Charles L. Lewis, *David Glasgow Farragut* (2 vols., Annapolis, 1941–1943), II, 138.

12. Seward to Tassara, May 21, 1863, FO 5/1096; Tassara to Seward, April 16, 1863, *Correspondence relative to the Steamer General Rusk,* p. 345; Koerner to Seward, April 18, 1863, Despatches from United States Ministers to Spain, XLV, Roll 44.

13. Lyons to Seward, August 1, 1863, and Seward to Lyons, August 4, 1863, *PRFA,* 1862/63, I, 612–613, 617–618; Lyons to Seward, October 29, 1863, and Seward to Frederick W. A. Bruce, March 27, 1866, FO 5/1096; Seward to Lyons, January 21, 1864, and Lyons to

Seward, June 13, 1864, *PRFA*, 1864, II, 498–499, 635–636; Seward to Bruce, August 3, 1866, Notes from the Department of State, Roll 43, pp. 51–52; Benjamin to John Slidell, March 26, 1863, *A Compilation of the Messages and Papers of the Confederacy*, ed. James D. Richardson (2 vols., Nashville, 1906), II, 464–465; "Report of Robert S. Hale, Esq.," *PRFA*, 1873, III, 51–52.

14. William G. Romaine to Milne, January 18, 1862, Adm. 13/31; Russell to Admiralty, January 31, 1862, MLN/P/B1(k), Milne Papers.

15. Welles to Lardner, August 6, 1862, Letterbook LXXI, Gideon Welles Papers, Library of Congress.

16. *Diary of Gideon Welles*, ed. Howard K. Beale (3 vols., New York, 1960), I, 109; John S. Long, "The Wayward Commander: A Study of the Civil War Career of Charles Wilkes," Ph.D. dissertation, University of California, Los Angeles, 1953, p. 135; Welles to Wilkes, September 8 and 21, 1862, Containers 8 and 9, Charles Wilkes Papers, Library of Congress; Nassau *Guardian* quotation from *Shipping and Mercantile Gazette*, December 12, 1862.

17. Lyons to Seward, November 24, 1862, Adm. 128/58; Wilkes to Welles, January 2, 1863, *ORN*, Ser. 1, II, 8–9; Seward to Lyons, December 5, 1862, *PRFA*, 1862/63, I, 416–417; Welles to Wilkes, December 11, 1862, and Welles to Seward, December 3, 1862, Letterbook LXXII, Gideon Welles Papers, Library of Congress; and Welles to Wilkes, December 2, 1862, Container 11, Charles Wilkes Papers, Library of Congress.

18. Regis A. Courtemanche, "Vice Admiral Sir Alexander Milne, K.C.B., and the North American and West India Station, 1860–1864," Ph.D. dissertation, London School of Economics and Political Science, 1967, pp. 216–217; George J. Malcolm to Milne, November 24, 1862, Milne to Malcolm, December 16, 1862, Seward to Lyons, February 7, 1863, and Lyons to Seward, December 9, 1863, Adm. 128/59; Seward to Lyons, December 16, 1862, *PRFA*, 1862/63, I, 421; Welles to Wilkes, January 14, 1863, *ORN*, Ser. 1, II, 24.

19. Louis Rothe to Wilkes, April 10, 1863, and Wilkes to Rothe, May 13, 1863, *ORN*, Ser. 1, II, 149, 152; Autobiography of Charles Wilkes, p. 2357, Charles Wilkes Papers, Library of Congress.

20. The Danish note, lacking an addressee, signature, and a date, is found in Seward to Welles, June 5, 1863, Letterbook, LXXIV, Gideon Welles Papers, Library of Congress.

21. Welles to Seward, June 8, 1863, FO 5/937.

22. Lyons to Seward, May 4 and 7, 1863, *PRFA*, 1862/63, I, 523–526; Lyons to Russell, May 5, 1863, FO 5/937.

23. Lyons to Russell, May 11, 1863, PRO 30/22/37; Welles,

Diary, I, 298–299, 304–305, 322; London *Shipping and Mercantile Gazette*, June 13, 1863; William W. Jeffries, "The Civil War Career of Charles Wilkes," *Journal of Southern History*, XI (August, 1945), 347.

24. Welles to Lardner, June 1, 1863, *ORN*, Ser. 1, II, 250–252.

25. Lyons to Seward, June 16, 1863, FO 5/937; Seward to Lyons, July 29, 1863, and Russell to Stuart, September 16, 1863, FO 5/937; Lyons to Seward, June 18, 1863, Notes from the British Legation, LIII; Welles to Seward, July 25, 1863, Letterbook LXXIV, Gideon Welles Papers, Library of Congress.

26. Napoleon Collins to Welles, December 26, 1862, and Welles to Collins, May 18, 1863, *ORN*, Ser. 1, I, 598–599; Welles to Seward, January 17, 1863, and Thomas J. Boynton to Seward, February 2, 1863, Miscellaneous Letters, Roll 195, pp. 7, 8; The United States vs. The Schooner Mont Blanc and Cargo, Prize, Final Order, Miscellaneous Letters, Roll 202, p. 543; Lyons to Seward, May 1, 1863, and Seward to Lyons, May 7, 1863, *PRFA*, 1862/63, I, 522 and 528.

27. Collins to Welles, July 5, 1863, *ORN*, Ser. 1, I, 599–600; Welles to Seward, July 31, 1863, Miscellaneous Letters, Roll 202, pp. 538–542; Seward to Welles, August 4, 1863, Domestic Letters, LXI, 328–330; Seward to Lyons, August 8, 1864, Notes from the Department of State, Roll 40, pp. 570–571; Welles, *Diary*, I, 398–399, 409–410.

28. James M. Mason to Russell, July 6, 1863, and Lyons to Seward, March 21, 1864, *PRFA*, 1863/64, I, 779, II, 563; Stuart to Seward, September 12, 1864, *ibid.*, I, 624–625; Nassau *Guardian*, June 3, 1863; *Standard*, July 4, 1863; *Army and Navy Gazette*, July 4, 1863; *Shipping and Mercantile Gazette*, July 15, 1863.

29. Welles to Seward, April 2, 1864, Miscellaneous Letters, Roll 211, p. 18; *Proceedings of a Court of Inquiry in the case of Commander Stephen D. Trenchard, Commanding the U.S. Steamer Rhode Island, charged with violating the territorial jurisdiction of Great Britain by pursuing and firing into the British Steamer Margaret and Jessie within said Jurisdiction* (Washington, D.C., 1864), p. 24.

30. Palmer, Robert P. Collier, and Phillimore to Russell, August 11, 1864, FO 83/222; J. Hume Burnley to Seward, September 10, 1864, *PRFA*, 1863/64, II, 704–705.

31. Welles to Seward, October 15, 1862, Gideon Welles, *Lincoln and Seward* (New York, 1874), pp. 169–171; Perry to Seward, September 15, 1863, Despatches from United States Ministers to Spain, XLV, Roll 44.

32. Seward to Burnley, September 16, 1864, *PRFA*, 1864, II, 708–709.

33. Romaine to Austin H. Layard, November 15, 1864, and
J. Emerson Tennant to Layard, November 18, 1864, FO 5/1234;
Palmer, Collier, and Phillimore to Russell, September 27, 1865.

8. THE EMILY ST. PIERRE: ONE THAT GOT AWAY

1. William J. Potts, "Biographical Sketch of the Hon. Thomas
H. Dudley of Camden, N.J.," *Proceedings of the American Philo-
sophical Society*, XXXIV (1895), 112, 117–118, 130; Charles Francis
Adams, Diary, May 4, 1862, Microfilm Roll 77, from the microfilms
of The Adams Papers, owned by the Adams Manuscript Trust and
deposited in the Massachusetts Historical Society; William H. Seward
to Charles F. Adams, May 1, 1862, Great Britain, House of Commons,
Sessional Papers, LXXII, 1863, North America, No. 4, "Despatch from
Her Majesty's Minister at Washington, Dated December 8th, 1862,
Inclosing Extracts of Papers Relating to Foreign Affairs, Presented
to Congress, December, 1862," p. 73; Jay Monaghan, *Diplomat in
Carpet Slippers: Abraham Lincoln Deals with Foreign Affairs* (Indianapolis, 1945), p. 339.

2. *The Journal of Benjamin Moran, 1857–1865*, ed. Sarah A. Wallace and Frances E. Gillespie (2 vols., Chicago, 1948, 1949), II, 982;
Virgil Carrington Jones, *The Civil War at Sea* (5 vols., New York,
1960), II, 242.

3. Adams to Seward, April 24, 1862, United States Department
of State, Despatches from United States Ministers to Great Britain,
LXXIX; Adams, Diary, April 21, 22, 1862, Roll 77; Moran, *Journal*,
II, 980–981; Francis H. Upton, *The Law of Nations Affecting Commerce During War* (New York, 1863), pp. 257–258.

4. Charleston *Mercury*, April 11 and May 26, 1862; John R.
Goldsborough to Gideon Welles, March 18, 1862, *ORN*, Ser. 1, XII,
636.

5. Liverpool *Post*, May 5, 1862; Charleston *Mercury*, May 26,
1862; Great Britain, House of Commons, *Sessional Papers*, "Papers
respecting the 'Emily St. Pierre,' of Liverpool," North America, No.
11, 1862, LXII, 2; Liverpool *Courier*, May 10, 1862.

6. Liverpool *Post*, June 5, 1862.

7. H. W. Muldaw to Welles, July 23, 1863, *PRFA*, 1862/63, I,
616.

8. Welles to Seward, March 8, 1862, Miscellaneous Letters, Roll
189, p. 85; Samuel F. Du Pont to Welles, May 14, 1862, *ORN*, Ser. 1,
XII, 814–815; Welles to Seward, May 20, 1862, *PRFA*, 1861/62,
p. 97; Seward to Adams, May 9, 1862, Diplomatic Instructions of the

Department of State, XVIII, 184; Seward to Welles, May 21, 1862, Domestic Letters, LVII, 244.

9. Adams to John Russell, April 24, 1862, Great Britain, Foreign Office, "Correspondence between Great Britain and the United States, relative to the Capture by United States Cruizers, of the British Vessel *Emily St. Pierre*, for an alleged attempt to break the blockade of Charleston; to her subsequent recapture by her Captain; and to the demand made by the United States' Government for her Restoration. —1862," *British and Foreign State Papers* (164 vols., London, 1812–1960), LV (1864–1865), 817–818 (hereafter cited as "Correspondence relative to the *Emily St. Pierre*").

10. Russell to Adams, May 7, 1862, *ibid.*, 818–819.

11. Adams to Russell, May 10, 1862, *ibid.*, 819–821. Adams' interpretation of the proclamation was also that of Francis H. Upton, a contemporary authority on prize law, who wrote caustically on the case in his *Law of Nations Affecting Commerce During War*, pp. 257–258.

12. Russell to Adams, May 24, 1862, "Correspondence relative to the *Emily St. Pierre*," 822–824.

13. Adams, Diary, May 26, 1862, Roll 77. Italics mine.

14. Adams, Diary, May 27, 1862, Roll 77; Adams to Russell, May 28, 1862, "Correspondence relative to the *Emily St. Pierre*," 824–828.

15. Adams to Russell, May 28, 1862, "Correspondence relative to the *Emily St. Pierre*," 829 and 831.

16. *Ibid.*, 831.

17. Russell to Adams, June 12, 1862, *ibid.*, 834–837.

18. Adams to Russell, June 13, 1862, *ibid.*, 837; Adams to Seward, June 13, 1862, Despatches from United States Ministers, LXXIX.

19. Russell to Adams, August 4, 1862, "Despatch from Her Majesty's Minister at Washington," 160–161.

20. Seward to Adams, August 25, 1862, *ibid.*, 171; Moran, *Journal*, II, 1022; Adams to Seward, June 18, 1862, Despatches from United States Ministers, LXXIX; Timothy Pickering to Robert Liston, May 3, 1800, quoted in Adams to Russell, July 7, 1862, Despatches from United States Ministers, LXXX.

21. Adams to Seward, June 18, 1862, *ibid.*, LXXIX; *Hansard's*, 3rd Ser., CLXVII, 724–725; Moran, *Journal*, II, 1023–1024.

9. THE TREATMENT OF NEUTRAL SUBJECTS

1. Richard B. P. Lyons to William H. Seward, November 7 and 30, 1861, Notes from the British Legation, XLII and XLIII; Gideon

Welles to Seward, November 30, 1861, Miscellaneous Letters, Roll 185, pp. 349–352; Alexander Milne to Lyons, December 7, 1861, and Lyons to John Russell, December 16, 1861, Adm. 128/56; Seward to Lyons, October 29, 1861, Notes from the Department of State, Roll 38, pp. 35–37.

2. Lyons to Seward, March 8, 1862, Notes from the British Legation, XLIII; Lyons to Seward, March 7 and May 26, 1863, and Seward to Lyons, April 2, 1863, *PRFA*, 1862/63, I, 464, 481, 553.

3. P. Edwards to Lyons, June 5, 1862, and William Stuart to Seward, August 1, 1862, Notes from the British Legation, XLIV and XLV; Welles to Seward, August 18, 1862, Miscellaneous Letters, Roll 192, pp. 274–289; William Atherton, Roundell Palmer, and Robert J. Phillimore to Russell, September 30, 1862, FO 83/2214.

4. Stuart to Seward, July 26, 1862, Notes from the British Legation, XLV; Samuel F. Du Pont to Welles, July 10, 1862, *ORN*, Ser. 1, XIII, 181–183; Seward to Stuart, November 12, 1862, and Lyons to Seward, February 17, 1863, *PRFA*, 1862/1863, I, 407, 454; Phillimore to Russell, November 28, 1862, FO 83/2215; Lyons to Russell, January 12, 1864, Private Letter Books, RBI, Lyons Papers, Arundel Castle, Sussex.

5. Welles to Louis M. Goldsborough, January 4, 1862, *ORN*, Ser. 1, VI, 498; Seward to Lyons, January 7, 1862, *PRFA*, 1861/62, pp. 242–243.

6. General Orders No. 41, June 10, 1862, *OR*, Ser. 1, XV, 484; James Parton, *General Butler in New Orleans* (New York, 1864), pp. 454–460.

7. Fred H. Harrington, *Fighting Politician: Major General N. P. Banks* (Philadelphia, 1948), p. 128; Private Journal No. 1, pp. 368–369, David Dixon Porter Papers, Library of Congress; Seward to Stanton, June 24, 1862; Henry W. Halleck to Benjamin F. Butler, August 28, 1862; General Orders, No. 82, July 21, 1862, *OR*, Ser. 1, XV, 497, 557, Ser. 3, II, 234–235; Harold M. Hyman, *Era of the Oath: Northern Loyalty Tests During the Civil War and Reconstruction* (Philadelphia, 1954), p. 39; Lyons to Seward, June 29 and August 28, 1864, *PRFA*, 1864, II, 643–644, 671; Welles to Seward, December 22, 1864, Miscellaneous Letters, Roll 219, p. 825.

8. Lyons to Russell, June 6, 1862, PRO 30/22/36; Welles to Robert Murray, May 26, 1862, Miscellaneous Letters, Roll 191, p. 480; Welles to Ganett J. Pendergrast, July 26, 1862, Letterbook LXXI, Gideon Welles Papers, Library of Congress; General Order of Acting Rear-Admiral Theodorus Bailey, January 1, 1863, *ORN*, Ser. 1, XVII, 342.

9. *Proceedings of a Naval General Court-Martial, in the case of Acting Master Alfred Everson, United States Navy, Charged with Assault with Intent to kill James O'Neill, a Fireman of the British Steamer Nicholas I, and with Maltreatment & Cruelty* (Washington, D.C., 1864), pp. 61–63, 71.

10. *Ibid.*, pp. 61, 67–68; Lyons to Seward, February 17 and 27, 1864, Notes from the British Legation, Roll 60.

11. Lyons to Seward, April 5, 1864, *PRFA*, 1864, II, 574; Palmer, Robert P. Collier, and Phillimore to Russell, April 6, 1864, FO 83/2221.

12. *Proceedings of a Naval General Court-Martial, in the case of Acting Master Alfred Everson*, pp. 1–3, 21, 25, 41, 44, 49, 57; J. Hume Burnley to Seward, October 18, 1864, Notes from the British Legation, Roll 71, LXXI.

13. Bailey to Aubrey G. Butterfield, June 17, 1863, and Russell to Lyons, March 25, 1864, FO 5/1005; George W. Ardill Statement, June 26, 1863, *ORN*, Ser. 1, II, 226; Lyons to Seward, July 17, and October 31, 1863; Seward to Stuart, October 9, 1863; Seward to Lyons, January 23, 1864, *PRFA*, 1862/63, I, 599–602, 631–633; 1864, II, 395, 501–503; Palmer, Collier, and Phillimore to Russell, March 18, 1864, FO 83/2220.

14. Lyons to Russell, July 20, 1863, FO 5/891; Lincoln to Welles, July 25, 1863, *ORN*, Ser. 1, II, 411; Welles to The President, September 30, 1863, Letterbook, LXXV, 63–66, Gideon Welles Papers, Library of Congress.

15. John Watson to Edward M. Archibald, December 14, 28, and 29, 1863, FO 5/1149; Edwin M. Stanton to Seward, December 12, 1863, Miscellaneous Letters, Roll 207, p. 239.

16. Seward to Lyons, January 29, 1864, and Lyons to Seward, April 25, 1864, *PRFA*, 1864, II, 509–510, 574.

17. Lyons to Russell, January 26 and May 23, 1864, Private Letter Books, RBI, Lyons Papers, Russell to Lyons, February 20, 1864, PRO 30/33/97; Lyons to Russell, May 9, 1864, PRO 30/22/38.

18. A full argument against the blockade-runners is given in Levi C. Turner to James A. Hardie, June 4, 1864, *OR*, Ser. 2, VII, 194–195.

19. Seward to Welles and Welles to S. P. Lee, January 11, 1864, *ORN*, Ser. 1, IX, 284–286, 405; Welles to Murray, January 11, 1864, Miscellaneous Letters, Roll 208, p. 655.

20. Lyons to Seward and Seward to Lyons, January 23, 1864, *PRFA*, 1864, II, 504, 506–507; New York *Herald*, January 18, 1864.

21. Charles F. Adams to Russell, January 25, 1864, FO 5/1149;

Adams to Russell, March 15 and April 16, 1864, *PRFA*, 1864, I, 330–331, 634–635; Russell to Adams, March 9, April 11, June 18, 1864, *PRFA*, I, 328, 634; II, 183; Adams to Russell, June 20, 1864, in Adams to Seward, June 23, 1864, Despatches from United States Ministers to Britain, Roll 83, LXXXVII.

22. Lyons to Russell, May 3, 1864, FO 5/1151; Lyons to Russell, May 23, 1864, FO 5/1152.

23. Welles to United States marshals, commanders of squadrons, and commanders of yards, May 9, 1864, *PRFA*, II, 630–631.

24. Collier, Palmer, and Phillimore to Russell, July 12, 1864, FO 83/2221.

25. Welles to Seward, May 13, 1864, in Seward to Lyons, May 16, 1864, *PRFA*, 1864, II, 609–610.

26. Seward to Lyons, May 31, 1864, *PRFA*, 621–622.

27. Palmer, Collier, and Phillimore to Russell, February 20, 1864, FO 83/2220; Seward to Lyons, February 19, 1864, and Deposition of Horace Carrew, February 19, 1864, in Russell to Lyons, February 20, 1864, *PRFA*, 1864, I, 306; II, 523; London *Standard*, February 14, 1864; *Manchester Guardian*, March 2, 1864.

28. Lyons to Seward, January 19, 1864, *PRFA*, 1864, I, 296; Welles to Seward, February 2 and March 2, 1864, Miscellaneous Letters, Roll 209, p. 30 and Roll 210, pp. 44–45; Lyons to Seward, February 13, 1864, Notes from the British Legation, LXI; Seward to Welles, February 27, 1864, Domestic Letters, LXIII, 318; *New York Times*, March 10, 1864.

29. *Proceedings of a Naval General Court Martial, in the case of Charles Danenhower, Acting Master's Mate, U.S. Navy, Charged with the Murder of James Gray, An Officer of the British Bark "Saxon"* (Washington, D.C., 1864), pp. 60–67.

30. *Ibid.*, p. 68; Seward to Lyons, June 22, 1864, and Russell to Lyons, August 11, 1864, FO 97/46.

31. Mary J. Gray to Russell, September 27, 1864, and Burnley to Russell, March 3, 1865, FO 97/46.

32. Seward to Burnley, February 27, 1865, FO 97/46.

33. Burnley to Seward, October 20 and November 26, 1864, *PRFA*, 1864, II, 745, 805–809.

34. Seward to Lyons, November 1, 1864, Notes from the Department of State, Roll 41, pp. 337–339; Palmer, Collier, and Phillimore to Russell, December 19, 1864, FO 83/2222.

35. Record of the proceedings of a Naval Court of Inquiry held at the Navy Yard *Boston*, Massachusetts to investigate the circum-

stances attending the capture and destruction of the steamer *Night Hawk* off Wilmington, N.C. September 30th 1864, pp. 55-61, Case Number 4522, Records of the Office of the Judge Advocate General (Navy), Records of the General Courts-Martial and Courts of Inquiry, 1799–1867, Record Group 125, National Archives.

36. Frederick W. A. Bruce to Seward, July 12, 1865, and Seward to Bruce, July 18, 1865, *PRFA*, 1865, II, 182–184.

37. *New York Times*, March 16, 1865.

38. *OR*, Ser. 1, XLVII, Part 3, p. 53; Burnley to Seward, March 16, 1865, and Seward to Burnley, March 17, 1865, *PRFA*, 1865, II, 99–100.

10. GREAT BRITAIN LOOKS AT THE PRIZE CASES

1. J. R. Pole, *Abraham Lincoln and the Working Classes of Britain* (London, 1952); Joseph H. Park, "The English Workingmen and the American Civil War," *Political Science Quarterly*, XXXIX (September, 1924), 432–457; Royden Harrison, "British Labour and the Confederacy," *International Review of Social History*, II (1951), 78–105; "The Opinion of the Middle Classes," *Saturday Review*, XV (January 31, 1863), 137–138; Arnold Whitridge, "British Liberals and the American Civil War," *History Today*, XII (October, 1962), 688–695; Wilbur D. Jones, "The British Conservatives and the American Civil War," *American Historical Review*, LVIII (April, 1953), 527–543; John O. Waller, "Attitudes (1860–1865) of Certain Representative English Men of Letters on the American Civil War," M.A. thesis, University of Southern California, 1949; Robert L. Duffus, "Contemporary English Popular Opinion on the American Civil War," M.A. thesis, Stanford University, 1911; Ephraim D. Adams, *Great Britain and the American Civil War* (2 vols., New York, 1925); Henry D. Jordan, "England and the War of Secession: A Study of Contemporary Opinion," Ph.D. dissertation, Harvard University, 1925; Max Beloff, "Great Britain and the American Civil War," *History*, XXVII (February, 1952), 40–48; Kenneth Bourne, *Britain and the Balance of Power in North America, 1815–1918* (Berkeley, 1967), pp. 251–312; Joseph M. Hernon, Jr., "British Sympathies in the American Civil War: A Reconsideration," *Journal of Southern History*, XXXIII (August, 1967), 356–367; Robert H. Jones, "Anglo-American Relations, 1861–1865, Reconsidered," *Mid-America: An Historical Review*, XLV (January, 1963), 36–49; Martin P. Claussen, "Peace Factors in Anglo-American Relations, 1861–1865," *Mississippi Valley Historical Review*, XXVI (March, 1940), 511–522; Amos Khasigian, "Economic Factors and British Neutrality, 1861–1865," *Historian*, XXV (August, 1963), 451–465; Louis B. Schmidt, "The Influence of

Wheat and Cotton on Anglo-American Relations During the Civil War," *Iowa Journal of History and Politics*, XVI (July, 1918), 400–439; Eli Ginsberg, "The Economics of British Neutrality during the American Civil War," *Agricultural History*, X (October, 1936), 147–156; Henry B. Smith, "British Sympathy with America, A Review of the Course of the Leading Periodicals of Great Britain upon the Rebellion in America," *American Presbyterian Review* (July, 1862), 487–532; George H. Putnam, "The London *Times* and the American Civil War," *Putnam's Magazine*, V (November, 1908), 183–191; Sarah A. Wallace, "Public Opinion in Great Britain on the American Civil War, 1861–1865 as Shown in the London Times," Ph.D. dissertation, American University, 1925; Joseph M. Hernon, Jr., *Celts, Catholics, and Copperheads: Ireland Views the American Civil War* (Cleveland, 1967).

2. *Shipping and Mercantile Gazette*, October 21, 1861; March 26, 1863; April 21 and 23, 1863; February 29, 1864.

3. *The Times* (London), August 9 and October 28, 1862; April 16 and 21; May 4 and 20; June 30; August 20, 1863.

4. *Standard*, March 28, April 22, and June 17, 1863; Henry Hotze to Judah P. Benjamin, April 25, 1862, box 7, folder 70, Confederate States of America, State Department Records, Library of Congress.

5. *Morning Post*, April 23 and 24; June 17, 1863.

6. *Globe and Traveller*, April 6, 1863; *Daily News*, April 23 and 28, 1863; *Army and Navy Gazette*, August 23, 1862; *Spectator*, May 10, 1862; *Economist*, April 4, 1863.

7. *Liverpool Courier*, April 1, 11, 27, 28; May 4; June 5; July 2, 1863.

8. *Liverpool Mercury*, March 23, April 22, May 22, 1862.

9. *Gore's General Advertiser*, April 2 and 30, 1863.

10. *Manchester Guardian*, April 23 and 27; May 1, 1863; *Southampton Times*, April 25, 1863; *Falmouth and Penryn Weekly Times and General Advertiser*, April 25, 1863; *Sheffield and Rotherham Independent*, April 25, 1863.

11. *Newcastle Daily Chronicle*, April 25 and 29, 1863; *Aris's Birmingham Gazette*, April 25, 1863; *Birmingham Journal*, May 2, 1863.

12. *Hansard's Parliamentary Debates* (3rd Series, 356 vols., London, 1830–1891), CLXX, 1819–1821, CLXXIII, 504, 516–517, 524; Frank L. Owsley, *King Cotton Diplomacy* (Chicago, 1931), pp. 246, 464, 466; Ephraim D. Adams, *Great Britain and the American Civil War* (2 vols., London, 1925), II, 25, 187, and 193.

13. Wilbur D. Jones, "The British Conservatives and the American Civil War," *American Historical Review*, LVIII (April, 1953), 537–542.

14. John Bigelow to William H. Seward, April 23, 1863, Letters, 1862–1866, John Bigelow Papers, New York Public Library; James M. Mason to Judah P. Benjamin, April 27, 1863, James M. Mason Papers, IX, Library of Congress.

15. Lyons to Russell, April 13, 1863, Copies of Despatches, RA–4; Lyons to Russell, April 13, 1863, and Lyons to Alexander Milne, May 11, 1863, Private Letter Books, RBI, Lyons Papers, Arundel Castle, Sussex; Lyons to Russell, April 21, 1863, Russell Papers, PRO 30/22/37.

16. Richard Cobden to Charles Sumner, May 22, 1863, Richard Cobden Papers #43676, p. 233, British Museum.

17. Francis Deák and Philip C. Jessup, *A Collection of Neutrality Laws, Regulations and Treaties of Various Countries* (2 vols., Washington, D.C., 1939), I, 165; Palmerston to Russell, October 10, 1861, Palmerston Papers, GC/RU/1139/2, National Register of Archives, used by permission of the Trustees of the Broadlands Archives; *Hansard's*, CLXXIII, 530.

18. William Atherton and Roundell Palmer to Russell, June 27, 1862, Law Officers' Reports, FO 83/2214; James P. Baxter, III, "The British Government and Neutral Rights, 1861–1865," *American Historical Review*, XXXIV (October, 1928), 29; Frank O. Gatell, "Great Britain and the Civil War Blockade," *Historia*, VII (1957), 40–41.

19. Earl Russell, *Recollections and Suggestions* (London, 1875), p. 276; Russell to Palmerston, August 24, 1862, Palmerston Papers, GC/RU/724/1–2.

20. *Hansard's*, CLXX, 1827–1831; Edmund Hammond to James Spense, April 3, 1863, *The Times*, April 7, 1863; Austin H. Layard to James Horsfall, July 5, 1862, Great Britain, House of Commons, *Sessional Papers*, LXXII, 1863, North America, No. 4, "Despatch from Her Majesty's Minister at Washington, Dated December 8th, 1862, Inclosing Extracts of Papers Relating to Foreign Affairs, Presented to Congress, December, 1862," p. 160; Russell to Lyons, April 25, June 13 and 20, 1863, and Russell to William Stuart, September 18, 1863, Russell Papers, PRO 30/22/97.

21. Russell to Lyons, April 8, 1861, Russell Papers, PRO 30/22/22; Lyons to Russell, July 20 and October 26, 1863, Russell Papers, PRO 30/22/37; Lyons to Earl of Mulgrave, August 3, 1863, and Lyons to Russell, July 29, 1864, Private Letter Books, RBI, Lyons Papers.

22. Lyons to Stuart, July 5, 1862, Private Letter Books, RBI, Lyons Papers.

23. Duke of Somerset and F. W. Grey to George Rodney, February 3, 1864, Adm. 13/5.

24. Lyons to Russell, October 16, 1863, Foreign Office, General Correspondence, United States of America, Series II, FO 5/894; *The Diary of Gideon Welles,* ed. Howard K. Beale (3 vols., New York, 1960), I, 468; *Army and Navy Gazette,* December 3, 1863; C. Paget to Alexander Milne, April 8, 1864; James T. Paddock to Milne, June 28, 1864; Philip C. Hill to Milne, November 9, 1863; Seward to Lyons, December 3, 1863, MLN/P/C/1(C).

25. Standing Orders for British squadron on North America and West India Station, July 1, 1862, Adm. 13/184; Milne Memo, September 9, 1862, Adm. 128/56; Supplemental Instructions for Cruizers employed on the Coast of America, November 12, 1861, Adm. 128/56; Milne to Watson, August 8, 1862, Adm. 128/58; Regis A. Courtemanche, "Vice Admiral Sir Alexander Milne, K. C. B., and the North American and West India Station, 1860–1864," Ph.D. dissertation, London School of Economics and Political Science, 1967, pp. 42, 188, 251; Milne to Watson, August 28, 1862, and Milne to Evart, September 29, 1862, MLN/107/3.

A Note on the Sources

THIS study is based on a variety of court records, diplomatic correspondence, naval reports, and papers of central figures; on public opinion as reflected in the comments of observers, journals, and debates in Parliament and in Congress; and on analyses of the legal, diplomatic, and naval aspects of the Civil War prize cases.

Before the present examination of the cases was made, Frank L. Owsley provided the only general study—"America and Freedom of the Seas, 1861–65," in *Essays in Honor of William E. Dodd,* ed. Avery Craven (Chicago, 1935), 194–256. While it is not comprehensive and while it does contain inaccuracies and some debatable points, the Owsley paper pioneered the subject and was useful. Madeline Robinton, *An Introduction to the Papers of the New York Prize Court, 1861–1865* (New York, 1945) is basic to an understanding of prize procedures. Especially useful for its detailed analysis of the diplomacy and legal evolution of the Union blockade is Sister Mary M. O'Rourke, "The Diplomacy of William H. Seward During the Civil War: His Policies as Related to International Law," Ph.D. dissertation, University of California,

Berkeley, 1963. Other works useful to an understanding of the Union blockade and prize procedures are Anonymous, "Blockade," *United States Naval Institute Proceedings*, XI (1885), 423–463; Francis B. C. Bradlee, *Blockade Running during the Civil War and the Effect of Land and Water Transportation on the Confederacy* (Salem, Massachusetts, 1925); James D. Bulloch, *The Secret Service of the Confederate States in Europe or How the Confederate Cruisers were Equipped* (2 vols., New York, 1959); Hamilton Cochran, *Blockade Runners of the Confederacy* (Indianapolis, 1958); Paul Hendren, "The Confederate Blockade Runners," *United States Naval Institute Proceedings*, LIX (April, 1933), 506–512; W. R. Hooper, "Blockade-running," *Harper's New Monthly Magazine*, XLII (December, 1870), 105–108; Virgil C. Jones, *The Civil War at Sea* (3 vols., New York, 1960); James M. Merrill, *The Rebel Shore* (Boston, 1957); Bradley S. Osbon, *Handbook of the U.S. Navy; Being a Compilation of Main Events of Every U.S. Naval Vessel, April, 1861–May, 1864* (New York, 1864); A. Sellow Roberts, "High Prices and the Blockade in the Confederacy," *South Atlantic Quarterly*, XXIV (April, 1925), 154–163; Horatio L. Wait, "The Blockade of the Confederacy," *Century Magazine* (July, 1898), 914–928; Richmond *Dispatch*, June 3, 1864; and William Watson, *The Adventures of a Blockade Runner; or, Trade in Time of War* (London, 1892).

The viewpoints of the Navy Department and its officers, and many of the details of the prize cases, are found in United States Navy Department, *Official Records of the Union and Confederate Navies in the War of the Rebellion* (29 vols., Washington, D.C., 1894–1922), which may be supplemented by Letters to Officers Commanding Squadrons or Vessels, Record Group 45, National Archives. Naval court investigations and trials of officers who got themselves into serious trouble with England are located in: *Proceedings of a Court of Inquiry in the case of Commander Stephen D. Trenchard, Commanding the U.S. Steamer Rhode Island, charged with violating the territorial jurisdiction of Great Britain by pursuing and firing into the British Steamer Margaret and Jessie within said Jurisdiction* (Washington, D.C., 1864);

"Record of the proceedings of a Naval Court of Inquiry held at the Navy Yard *Boston*, Mass. to investigate the circumstances attending the capture and destruction of the steamer *Night Hawk* off Wilmington, N.C. September 30th 1864," Case Number 4522, Records of the Office of the Judge Advocate General (Navy), Records of the General Courts-Martial and Courts of Inquiry, 1799–1867, Record Group 125, National Archives; *Proceedings of a Naval General Court Martial, in the Case of Charles Danenhower, Acting Master's Mate, U.S. Navy, Charged with the Murder of James Gray, An Officer of the British Bark "Saxon"* (Washington, D.C., 1864); and *Proceedings of a Naval General Court-Martial, in the case of Acting Master Alfred Everson, United States Navy, Charged with Assault with Intent to kill James O'Neill, a Fireman of the British Steamer Nicholas I, and with Maltreatment and Cruelty* (Washington, D.C., 1864). The dogmatic and patriotic Secretary of the Navy has left historians much lively and valuable reading: *The Diary of Gideon Welles*, ed. Howard K. Beale (3 vols., New York, 1960), and the Gideon Welles Papers, located in the Library of Congress and in the Henry E. Huntington Memorial Library, San Marino, California. Also important are the Papers of Charles Wilkes, Library of Congress, and two highly critical studies: William W. Jeffries, "The Civil War Career of Charles Wilkes," *Journal of Southern History*, XI (August, 1945), 324–348, and John S. Long, "The Wayward Commander: A Study of the Civil War Career of Charles Wilkes," Ph.D. dissertation, University of California, Los Angeles, 1953. The relevant thoughts of other naval officers are anchored in the David Dixon Porter Papers, Library of Congress; Charles L. Lewis, *David Glasgow Farragut* (2 vols., Annapolis, 1941–1943); John S. Barnes, "My Egotistigraphy: The Egotistigraphy of a Rolling Stone, that gathered Moss, herein scraped off for the information and amusement of his family," typescript copy, 1910, New York Historical Society Library; Albert Gleaves, "The Affair of the Blanche," *United States Naval Institute Proceedings*, XLVIII (October, 1922), 1661–1676.

The most comprehensive collection of lower court records is *The Federal Cases, Comprising Cases Argued and Determined in the Circuit and District Courts of the United States* (30 vols., St. Paul, Minnesota, 1894–1897), but other pertinent materials include Samuel R. Betts, *The Blockade, Opinion of Hon. Samuel R. Betts, Judge of the U.S. District Court for the Southern District of N.Y., in the cases of The Hiawatha and other vessels captured as prize* (New York, 1861); United States District Court, Southern District of New York, *United States of America against The Hiawatha and Her Cargo, Argument of Mr. Charles Edwards, in the case of the British Barque Hiawatha, as Advocate for Owners of the Vessel and portion of her Cargo, and also for H.B.M.'s Consul at New York, intervening for absent British Owners of other parts* (New York, 1861), and the same court's *The United States v. The Steamer Peterhoff and Her Cargo, in Prize, Opinion of the Court, by Judge Betts* (New York, 1864); The Steamer *Labuan*, Case Number 71, and The Steamer *Peterhoff*, Case Number 151, on microfilm at Columbia University; United States District Court, Massachusetts, *Decisions of Hon. Peleg Sprague, 1841–64*, ed. Richard Henry Dana (2 vols., Boston, 1868).

Supreme Court verdicts and the most important arguments are presented in John W. Wallace, *Cases argued and adjudged in the Supreme Court of the United States, 1863–1874* (23 vols., Washington, D.C., 1874–1875); Samuel F. Miller, *Reports of Decisions in the Supreme Court of the United States* (4 vols., Washington, D.C., 1874–1875); and the *U.S. Supreme Court Reports, Cases Argued and Decided in the Supreme Court of the United States*, Lawyers' Edition (118 vols., Rochester, 1917–1967), which includes arguments left out of the other published collections. Other useful items are: Supreme Court of the United States, Case Number 231, Rafael Preciat, Claimant of the Mexican Schooner Brilliant and Cargo, Appellant, vs. The United States, Appeal from the District Court of the United States for the Southern District of Florida; and Mr. Sedgwick's Brief for the Captors (n.p., n.d.), in U.S. Supreme Court, Records and Briefs, 2 *Black* 613–672, Library of Congress Law Library.

Skeletal information on the disposition of postwar prize claims is in Mixed Commission on British and American Claims,

List of Claims of British Subjects against the United States, and American Citizens against Great Britain, before the Mixed Commission under the Twelfth Article of the Treaty of Washington of May 8, 1871 (Washington, D.C., 1873) and United States Department of State, *Papers Relating to the Treaty of Washington* (6 vols., Washington, D.C., 1874). Opinions of the reasons for the verdicts are occasionally given in the "Report of Robert S. Hale, Agent and Counsel of the United States before the Commission on Claims of Citizens of the United States against Great Britain, and of Subjects of Her Britannic Majesty against the United States, under the Twelfth Article of the Treaty of 8th May, 1871, between the United States and Great Britain," in United States Department of State, *Diplomatic Correspondence, Papers Relating to Foreign Affairs*, 1873, III, 1–260.

Special attention is given to maritime law in Sir Robert Phillimore, *Commentaries upon International Law* (4 vols., London, 1854–1861); E. S. Roscoe, *Reports of Prize Cases Determined in the High Court of Admiralty from 1754–1859* (2 vols., London, 1905); Francis H. Upton, *The Law of Nations Affecting Commerce During War: with a Review of Jurisdiction, Practice and Proceedings of Prize Courts* (New York, 1863); Carlton Savage, *Policy of the United States Toward Maritime Commerce in War* (2 vols., Washington, D.C., 1934); John B. Moore, *A Digest of International Law* (8 vols., Washington, D.C., 1906); Charles C. Hyde, *International Law Chiefly as Interpreted by the United States* (3 vols., Boston, 1945); and J. M. Kenworthy and George Young, *Freedom of the Seas* (New York, 1928).

The doctrine of continuous voyage is analyzed and evaluated in Llewellyn A. Atherly-Jones, *Commerce in War* (London, 1907); Thomas E. Baker, "Contraband of War," Ph.D. dissertation, Harvard University, 1947; Thomas Baty, "Continuous Voyage as applied to Blockade and Contraband," *Transactions of The Grotius Society*, XX (London, 1935), and also in his edited *Prize Law and Continuous Voyage; containing Brief in the Springbok case, by the Hon. W. M. Evarts, sometime state secretary. Analysis of the Springbok judgment, by D.C.L.* (London, 1915), which also includes Sir Travers Twiss, "The Doctrine of Continuous

210 · *Squall Across the Atlantic*

Voyage as applied to Contraband of War and Blockade, contrasted with the Declaration of Paris of 1856," pp. 6–30; Herbert W. Briggs, *The Doctrine of Continuous Voyage* (Baltimore, 1926); Norman Bentwich, *The Law of Private Property in War* (London, 1907); Charles B. Elliott, "The Doctrine of Continuous Voyages," *American Journal of International Law*, I (January, 1907), 61–104; Paul Fauchille, "La Théorie du Voyage Continu en Matière de Contrebande de Guerre," *Revue Générale de Droit International Public*, IV (1897), 297–323; James W. Gantenbein, *The Doctrine of Continuous Voyage, Particularly as Applied to Contraband and Blockade* (Portland, Oregon, 1929); Louis Gessner, *A Juridicial Review of the Case of the British Barque "Springbok"* (London, 1875); Charles N. Gregory, "The Doctrine of Continuous Voyage," *Harvard Law Review*, XXIV (January, 1911), 167–181; Alexander Holtzoff, "Some Phases of Law of Blockade," *American Journal of International Law*, X (January, 1916), 53–64; Anonymous, "The Law of Ulterior Destination as Bearing on Contraband of War," *Law Magazine and Review*, XXX (1870), 73–89; Harold R. Pyke, *The Law of Contraband of War* (London, 1915).

Bits and pieces of the *Peterhoff* story may be picked up in *The Journal of Benjamin Moran, 1857–1865*, ed. Sarah A. Wallace and Frances E. Gillespie (2 vols., Chicago, 1948, 1949); *The British Steam-Ship "Peterhoff," A Report of Her Seizure by the United States Cruiser "Vanderbilt," And The Subsequent Proceedings In The United States Prize Court, At New York. Before the Hon. Judge Betts* (New York, 1863), which was designed to influence Northern public opinion in favor of the claimants but is nevertheless useful because it contains source material for the early phases of the case; "U.S. vs. The British Steamer 'Peterhoff.' Contem. Cops. of letters on the above case from William H. Seward, Gideon Welles, A. Lincoln, Francis H. Upton, C. H. Baldwin, Chas. Wilkes & others," Gideon Welles Papers, Huntington Library; Gideon Welles, *Lincoln and Seward* (New York, 1874); and *The Collected Works of Abraham Lincoln*, ed. Roy P. Basler (9 vols., New Brunswick, New Jersey, 1953).

Particularly relevant to the *Prize Cases* are the *Arguments and Speeches of William Maxwell Evarts,* ed. Sherman Evarts (3 vols., New York, 1919); William M. Evarts Papers, Library of Congress; Miscellaneous Correspondence relative to disposition of vessels and property captured by U.S. ships, 1861–1865, folder 4711, XZ Prizes, prize money, and prize sales (legal and financial aspects), Record Group 45, National Archives; *The Statutes at Large of the United States of America, from the organization of the government in 1789 to concurrent resolutions of the two houses of Congress and recent treaties, conventions, and executive proclamations* (39 vols., Boston and Washington, D.C., 1845–1919); Charles F. Adams, *Richard Henry Dana: A Biography* (2 vols., Cambridge, Massachusetts, 1890); Louis B. Boudin, *Government by Judiciary* (2 vols., New York, 1932); Edward S. Corwin, *The President: Office and Powers, 1787–1957* (New York, 1957); Brainerd Dyer, *The Public Career of William M. Evarts* (Berkeley, 1933); Charles G. Haines and Foster H. Sherwood, *The Role of the Supreme Court in American Government and Politics, 1835–1864* (2 vols., Berkeley and Los Angeles, 1957); George F. Milton, *The Use of Presidential Power, 1789–1943* (Boston, 1944); James G. Randall, *Constitutional Problems under Lincoln* (Urbana, 1951); Carl B. Swisher, *Stephen J. Field: Craftsman of the Law* (Washington, D.C., 1930), and *Roger B. Taney* (New York, 1935); and John M. Zane, *Lincoln the Constitutional Lawyer* (Springfield, Illinois, 1933).

Because of the small interest of the Attorneys General in the prize cases, the following works are of only limited value: *The Diary of Edward Bates, 1859–1866,* ed. Howard K. Beale, Annual Report of the American Historical Association for 1930, IV (Washington, D.C., 1933); Attorney General Papers, Letters Received, State Department, and Letterbooks, Record Group 60, National Archives; United States Department of Justice, *Official Opinions of the Attorneys General of the United States* (41 vols., Washington, D.C., 1852–1960).

Crucial to this study are the General Records of the Department of State, Record Group 59, National Archives; Notes from the Department of State to foreign ministers and consuls in the United States, Great Britain, 1834–1906; Notes from the British

212 · *Squall Across the Atlantic*

Legation in the United States, 1791–1906; Despatches from United States Ministers to Great Britain, 1791–1906; Despatches from United States Consuls in London, England, 1790–1906; Despatches from United States Consul in Liverpool, England, 1790–1906; Diplomatic Instructions of the Department of State, Great Britain, 1801–1906; Diplomatic Instructions of the Department of State, Spain, 1801–1906; and the correspondence of the State Department with other branches of the American government, the Domestic Letters and Miscellaneous Letters of the Department of State. Much but not all of the diplomatic correspondence is published in United States Department of State, *Diplomatic Correspondence, Papers Relating to Foreign Affairs* (239 vols., Washington, D.C., 1861–1969), and the same department's *Correspondence relative to the Steamer General Rusk, alias Blanche. To which is appended the proceedings of a court martial in the case of Commander Hunter* (Washington, D.C., 1863), which includes much important material for this case.

Convenient compilations of Civil War diplomatic correspondence focusing on other specific topics are in the House of Commons' *Sessional Papers:* "Papers respecting the 'Emily St. Pierre,' of Liverpool," North America No. 11, 1862, LXII; "Correspondence Respecting the Seizure of the British Schooner 'Will o' The Wisp' by the United States' Ship of War 'Montgomery,' at Matamoros, June 3, 1862," North America No. 12, 1862, LXXII; "Despatch from Her Majesty's Minister at Washington, Dated December 8th, 1862, Inclosing Extract of Papers Relating to Foreign Affairs, Presented to Congress, December, 1862," North America No. 4, 1863, LXXII; "Correspondence Respecting the seizure of the British vessels 'Springbok' and 'Peterhoff' by United States cruisers in 1863," CV 1900 (Cd. 34). Likewise useful are Great Britain, Parliament, "Correspondence respecting interference with trade between New York and the Bahamas," North America No. 14, 1863 (London, 1863); and Foreign Office, "Correspondence between Great Britain and The United States, relative to the Capture, by United States' Cruisers, of the British Vessel *Emily St. Pierre*, for an alleged attempt to break the Blockade of Charleston; to her subsequent Recapture by her

Captain; and to the demand made by the United States' Government for her Restoration—1862," *British and Foreign State Papers* (London, 164 vols., 1812–1960), LV (1864–1865), 817–837.

For the thinking of important representatives of the State Department, see the William Henry Seward Papers, Rush Rhees Library, University of Rochester, and Dexter Perkins, "William H. Seward as Secretary of State," in Union College, *Union Worthies Number Six, William H. Seward* (Schenectady, 1951), both of which are disappointing for the prize cases, especially when compared with the information found in the State Department records; The Adams Papers, owned by the Adams Manuscript Trust and deposited in the Massachusetts Historical Society, which includes on microfilm the Diary and Letterbooks of Charles Francis Adams; Martin B. Duberman, *Charles Francis Adams, 1807–1886* (Boston, 1960), an outstanding study; and the *Memoirs of Gustave Koerner, 1809–1896*, ed. Thomas J. McCormack (2 vols., Cedar Rapids, 1909), a useful work which favors the memorialist.

Sources for Northern opinion on the prize cases are scarce; military operations overwhelmingly upstaged those cases. Nevertheless, some Northern views of the cases are occasionally found in United States Congress, United States *Congressional Globe* (46 vols., Washington, D.C., 1834–1873); Boston *Transcript;* *Harper's Weekly;* Philadelphia *Public Ledger; Daily National Intelligencer;* New York *Daily Tribune;* and the *New York Times.*

Of some interest are Confederate States of America, State Department Records, Library of Congress; James M. Mason Papers, Library of Congress; *A Compilation of the Messages and Papers of the Confederacy*, ed. James D. Richardson (2 vols., Nashville, 1906); and the Charleston *Mercury* of April 11 and May 26, 1862, which has useful reports on the *Emily St. Pierre* case.

Aspects of the prize cases as viewed from the English side have been interpreted by a variety of observers and are located in the Letters, 1862–1866, of the John Bigelow Papers, New York Public Library; Regis A. Courtemanche, "Vice Admiral Sir Alexander Milne, K.C.B., and the North American and West India

Station, 1860–1864," Ph.D. dissertation, London School of Economics and Political Science, 1967; Richard Cobden Papers, British Museum; *A Cycle of Adams Letters, 1861–1865*, ed. Worthington C. Ford (2 vols., Boston, 1920); James P. Baxter, III, "The British Government and Neutral Rights, 1861–1865," *American Historical Review*, XXXIV (October, 1928), 9–29, and also his "Some British Opinions as to Neutral Rights, 1861 to 1865," *American Journal of International Law*, XXIII (July, 1929), 517–537; Frank O. Gatell, "Great Britain and the Civil War Blockade," *Historia*, VII (1957), 27–41; Douglas Maynard, "The Forbes-Aspinwall Mission," *Mississippi Valley Historical Review*, XLV (June, 1958), 67–89; Jay Monaghan, *Diplomat in Carpet Slippers: Abraham Lincoln Deals with Foreign Affairs* (Indianapolis, 1945); M. R. Pitt, "Great Britain and Belligerent Maritime Rights from the Declaration of Paris, 1856, to the Declaration of London, 1909," Ph.D. dissertation, University of London, 1964, an incomparable study; William J. Potts, "Biographical Sketch of the Hon. Thomas H. Dudley of Camden, N.J.," *Proceedings of the American Philosophical Society*, XXXIV (1895), 102–134; and Julius W. Pratt, "The British Blockade and American Precedents," *United States Naval Institute Proceedings*, XLVI (November, 1920), 1789–1802.

The views of Her Majesty's government and its key members are in Francis Deák and Philip C. Jessup, *A Collection of Neutrality Laws, Regulations and Treaties of Various Countries* (2 vols., Washington, D.C., 1939); Palmerston Papers, National Register of Archives, used by permission of the Trustees of the Broadlands Archives; Earl John Russell, *Recollections and Suggestions* (London, 1875); Russell Papers, PRO 30/22/, a disappointing collection located in the Public Record Office, London; Law Officers' Reports, FO 83/, Public Record Office; Foreign Office, General Correspondence, United States of America, Series II, FO 5/, a vital collection dealing with all aspects of the prize cases; Private Letter Books, RBI, Lyons Papers, Arundel Castle, Sussex; William Stuart Papers, PRO 30/36, Public Record Office; Admiralty 13/, Out Letters, and Admiralty 128/, North America and West Indies: Correspondence, Public Record Office;

Milne Papers, National Maritime Museum, Greenwich; James P. Baxter, III, "Papers Relating to Belligerent and Neutral Rights, 1861–1865," *American Historical Review*, XXXIV (October, 1928), 77–91.

The attitudes of members of Parliament and their constituents are recorded in *Hansard's* (3rd Series, 356 vols., London, 1830–1891); Frank L. Owsley, *King Common Diplomacy* (Chicago, 1931); Wilbur D. Jones, "The British Conservatives and the American Civil War," *American Historical Review*, LVIII (April, 1953), 527–543; and *The Dictionary of National Biography*, ed. Sir Leslie Stephen and Sir Sidney Lee (22 vols., London, 1921–1922). Public opinion is reflected in *The Times* (London), London *Daily News, Shipping and Mercantile Gazette, Economist, Morning Post, Spectator, Globe and Traveller, Saturday Review, Standard, Observer,* and *Army and Navy Gazette;* the *Liverpool Courier, Liverpool Mercury, Post,* and *Gore's General Advertiser of Liverpool;* and in the newspapers of other shipping and manufacturing centers: the *Manchester Guardian, Newcastle Daily Chronicle, Falmouth and Penryn Weekly Times and General Advertiser, Southampton Times, Aris's Birmingham Gazette, Birmingham Journal* and the *Sheffield and Rotherham Independent.*

Information useful to the study of the Matamoros–Brownsville trade and the prize cases which resulted from it is located in *Treaties and Other International Acts of the United States of America,* ed. Hunter Miller (8 vols., Washington, D.C., 1937); Anonymous, "The Last Battle of the War," *Southern Historical Society Papers,* XXI (1893), 226–227; Herbert Davenport, "Notes on Early Steamboating on the Rio Grande," *Southwestern Historical Quarterly,* LXIX (October, 1945), 286–289; Robert W. Delaney, "Matamoros, Port for Texas during the Civil War," *Southwestern Historical Quarterly,* LVIII (April, 1955), 473–487; Charles I. Evans, "Military Events and Operations in Texas and Along the Coasts and Border, 1861–1865," in Dudley G. Wooten, ed., *A Comprehensive History of Texas* (2 vols., Dallas, 1898), II, 519–570; Kathryn A. Hanna, "Incidents of the Confederate Blockade," *Journal of Southern History,* XI (May, 1945), 253–275; Charles W. Ramsdell, "Texas in the Confederacy," *The*

History of the Southern States, in *The South in the Building of the Nation* (12 vols., Richmond, 1909), III, 402–416, and his "The Texas State Military Board, 1862–1865," *Southwestern Historical Quarterly,* LVIII (April, 1955), 253–275; Leroy P. Graf, "The Economic History of the Lower Rio Grande Valley, 1820–1875," Ph.D. dissertation, 2 vols., Harvard University, 1942; Orville E. Avery, "Confederate Defense of Texas, 1861–1865," M.A. thesis, University of Oklahoma, 1940; Laura Snyder, "The Blockade of the Texas Coast During the Civil War," M.A. thesis, Texas Technological College, 1938; Bonnye R. Whitworth, "The Role of Texas in the Confederacy," M.A. thesis, North Texas State College, 1951; Robin W. Winks, *Canada and the United States: the Civil War Years* (Baltimore, 1960); Raphael Semmes, *Memoirs of Service Afloat During the War Between the States* (Baltimore, 1869); Don Niceto de Zamacois, *Historia de Méjico, Desde Sus Tiempos Mas Remotos Hasta Nuestros Dias* (22 vols., Barcelona, 1876–1902); Nannie M. Tillie, *Federals on the Frontier: The Diary of Benjamin F. McIntyre 1862–1864* (Austin, 1963). United States Department of the Army, *The War of the Rebellion: A Compilation of the Official Records of the Union and Confederate Armies* (128 vols., Washington, D.C., 1880–1901) is of value not only for the Matamoros cases, but also for other matters such as the treatment of neutrals.

Finally, Fred H. Harrington, *Fighting Politician: Major General N. P. Banks* (Philadelphia, 1948), Harold M. Hyman, *Era of the Oath: Northern Loyalty Tests During the Civil War and Reconstruction* (Philadelphia, 1954), and James Parton, *General Butler in New Orleans* (New York, 1864) touch upon the treatment of neutrals.

Index

control of U.S.-British trade, 15-17; occasions when intervened, 17; attitude toward using force, 39; demands reparations for *Labuan* seizure, 41-42; and U.S. use of continuous voyage doctrine, 67 (*see also* Continuous voyage); response to *Peterhoff* seizure, 67-68; reverses views on mail seizures, 72-73; refuses to intervene in *Springbok* case, 87, 93-94; evaluates French view of district court ruling on *Springbok* case, 87-88; outraged by *Blanche* incident, 104; angered by *Margaret and Jessie* affair, 114; opposes extinction of territorial jurisdiction, 116; criticizes *Night Hawk* inquiry findings, 147-148; fails to intervene forcefully in Civil War, 148, 149; urged to declare war, 156-159; desires neutrality, 159-160, 163-164; *see also below* and Lyons, Lord; Palmerston, Lord; Russell, Lord

Admiralty, British: orders naval force to protect British commerce, 39; moderate attitude of, 162; *see also* Milne, Alexander

Law officers of the Crown: accept Welles' analysis of limitations on belligerents, 56; analyze *Margaret and Jessie* case, 115; oppose extension of territorial jurisdiction, 116; response to new U.S. naval instructions, 142; favor belligerent proceedings, 160; mentioned, 54, 76, 87; see also *Science; Springbok*

Parliament: response to *Peterhoff* seizure in, 68-69; response to Adams' letter to Du Pont in, 74; criticism of British response to prize cases in, 156-157, 160, 163, 170

Grier, Robert C.: moved by Dana's argument, 27, 28; delivers Supreme Court majority opinion on *Prize Cases*, 29-30

Guadalupe Hidalgo, Treaty of: prevents blockade of Rio Grande, 36; relation to *Labuan* case, 37, 38

Guardian, Nassau, bemoans new command of Wilkes, 108

Halleck, Henry W., orders end to oaths for neutrals, 134

Hammond, Edmund, responds to Peterhoff's owner for Russell, 69

Hiawatha: identified, 21; early phases of case, 22-23; British response to, 23-24; Supreme Court condemns, 30; British government agrees to her guilt, 33

Hotze, Henry, propagandizes for Confederacy, 152

Hunter, Charles: seizes *Will o' the Wisp*, 47; Spanish minister asks for dismissal of, 103; to be relieved of command and tried, 103; trial of, 104

Index, London, mentioned, 152

Institute of International Law, criticizes Supreme Court ruling on *Springbok*, 91-92

International law: defined, 3n; and role of neutrals, 4; antebellum on neutrals' ships passing